More Praise for *Strategic Investing After 50* by Julie Jason

"A very good book. It is filled with practical investment advice that readers can easily understand and implement."

Philip Edwards, Managing Director, Standard and Poor's

"As an investment professional, I found Julie Jason's book to be an honest look at the risks as well as the rewards of the investment process, which are all too often ignored or misunderstood by financial advisers. This is a wonderfully clear, concise, and informstive guide for Boomers in their fifties and beyond."

Christopher S. Litchfield, Managing Partner, Stingray Partners

"This is a wonderful book. It is full of easy-to-understand advice on how to invest successfully. If my clients had read this book before they lost money, they would not have had the privilege of being my 'clients.'"

Seth E. Lipner, Esq., plaintiff's attorney and President, Public Investors Arbitration Bar Association

"If you are over 50 years old and you want to secure your future, Julie Jason maps it out for you . . . how to invest, what to invest in, and perhaps most importantly, when to sell. *Strategic Investing After 50* takes the mystery out of how to invest to secure your future, explaining investing concepts and strategies in plain English together with simple examples that are a cinch to follow. Julie also gives you a look at what your remedies are if you've had less than a sterling experience with your broker. Required reading for investors 50 years and older!"

Samantha Rabin, Senior Editor, Securities Arbitration Commentator

J.K. LASSER'S™

STRATEGIC INVESTING AFTER 50

Look for these and other titles from J.K. Lasser™—Practical Guides for All Your Financial Needs

J.K. Lasser's Pick Winning Stocks by Edward F. Mrkvicka, Jr.

J.K. Lasser's Invest Online by LauraMaery Gold and Dan Post

J.K. Lasser's Year-Round Tax Strategies by David S. De Jong and Ann Gray Jakabcin

J.K. Lasser's Taxes Made Easy for Your Home-Based Business by Gary W. Carter

J.K. Lasser's Finance and Tax for Your Family Business by Barbara Weltman

J.K. Lasser's Pick Winning Mutual Funds by Jerry Tweddell with Jack Pierce

J.K. Lasser's Your Winning Retirement Plan by Henry K. Hebeler

J.K. Lasser's Winning with Your 401(k) by Grace W. Weinstein

J.K. Lasser's Strategic Investing After 50 by Julie Jason

J.K. Lasser's Winning with Your 403(b) by Pam Horowitz

J.K. Lasser's Winning Financial Strategies for Women by Rhonda M. Ecker and Denise Gustin-Piazza

J.K. LASSER'S™

STRATEGIC INVESTING AFTER 50

Julie Jason

John Wiley & Sons, Inc.

New York • Chichester • Weinheim • Brisbane • Singapore • Toronto

Published by John Wiley & Sons, Inc.
Published simultaneously in Canada.

Library of Congress Cataloging-in-Publication Data:

Jason, Julie.
    J.K. Lasser's strategic investing after 50 / Julie Jason.
        p.   cm.
    Includes bibliographical references and index.
    ISBN 0-471-39779-2 (paper : alk. paper)
    1. Investments.   2. Finance, Personal.   3. Retirement income—Planning.
HG4521.J333   2001
332.024′01—dc21

                                                                2001024341

Printed in the United States of America.

10   9   8   7   6   5   4   3   2   1

To my students and readers, whose insightful
questions keep me learning.

And, to my clients,
whom I am honored to serve.

Contents

Preface

If you are near, at, or over 50, you grew up in a time when investment skills were not taught and rarely learned. The wealthy relied on professional advisers to manage their portfolios along with their other financial affairs. Other individuals may have picked a few stocks, bought some mutual funds, and invested personal savings in certificates of deposit, especially in the late 1970s and early 1980s when interest rates were particularly high.

Six dramatic changes in our lifetimes, however, not only have drawn more of us into the marketplace, but have also emphasized the need for success:

1. Commissions were deregulated in May 1975, opening the door for discounting and competition among brokerage firms.
2. Discounters discovered the Internet and made it exceptionally easy for individuals to open accounts and trade without leaving their homes.
3. The stock market began a bull run in 1982 that surpassed rational expectations, even after the 20 percent one-day decline of Black Monday, October 19, 1987.
4. Mutual fund investing grew dramatically.
5. The company-sponsored 401(k) plan arrived in the 1980s, in many cases displacing the company pension plan.
6. Demographics have shifted so that our generation will have more retirees receiving Social Security benefits than workers paying into the Social Security fund to support those benefits.

While each of these influences has impacted investor behavior, I would say that a combination of the last two—the dramatic increase in participant-directed 401(k) plans, and a realization about the limitations of private company pensions and Social Security in a society where people are living longer—are probably responsible for pushing the average American worker onto Wall Street. Drawing even the reticent into the stock market, the participant-directed 401(k) plan requires all eligible working Americans to have knowledge of investing and places the promises of the financial markets within their reach, irrespective of personal wealth. Assuming that these investors have the skill, knowledge, and discipline necessary to make profitable use of the markets, there are in fact, few barriers to success.

What we cannot assume is that skill, knowledge, and discipline come with age. Just as no sports fan can claim that watching the World Series prepares him to play for the Yankees, no amount of watching the financial news prepares a person for investing wisely. The Little League and local ball clubs weed out players before they make the big leagues. Unskilled investors are kept in the game until they lose all their money.

Learning to invest is experiential. You have to practice and learn from your mistakes, including how to deal with losses in a rational manner. It is more like learning how to play the piano, type, tap-dance, or swim.

Moreover, investing is not a competitive sport. In fact, it is not a sport at all, since winning against an opponent is not the objective. If the stock you picked beat the stock your brother picked, what does that prove? Except for boosting your ego, what does beating the Dow do for you?

Sound investing is a question of meeting your personal goals, whatever they may be. It is a matter of doing your "personal best" with the resources you have available.

As a personal money manager who also writes and teaches, I see the frustration of hard-working people who want to know how to invest wisely. Most do not have the luxury of taking a few years off to study the markets. Many learn from reading newspapers, magazines, and research reports, watching the financial news, or simply by jumping in and buying stocks. When you learn this way, you have to expect gaps in your knowledge and a few unanswered questions here and there. My reason for writing this book is to help you fill in some of those gaps and give you some insight and perspective about how to make good decisions at this time of life.

Since I started my career on Wall Street as a lawyer and serve occasionally as an arbitrator of investor disputes, I sometimes see things a little differently than many other financial advisers you might come across. In fact, after reading a draft of this manuscript, Ellie, one of my clients, asked me whether I disliked salespeople. While that is not the case, I do dislike opportunism at the expense of the client. I am certain that all the honest, reputable, and hard-working salespeople who may read this book will not disagree with what I have to say about the sales process. Because you may be investing large sums of money for the first time in your life, it is essential that you know the ropes before sitting down with a well-trained, highly skilled salesperson. I want to help you avoid buying something you don't understand, don't need, or can't get out of.

The organization of the book follows the flow of questions that are usually posed to me by my students. You will see some repetition as we move from one concept to another. This is intentional. I also use examples to illustrate different points. Although the names and identifying facts are fictional, these examples are based on real situations.

The essential lesson of *Strategic Investing After 50* is how to have your investments support you for the rest of your life without exposure to undue risk. First, I discuss why this time of life calls for a more thoughtful approach to investing (Chapter 1). Then, I list some common misconceptions many people have about investing (Chapter 2) and suggest more realistic expectations (Chapter 3). These three introductory chapters assume some knowledge of investing and do not contain definitions, which are developed in detail in Chapters 4 through 14.

There are 10 interdependent, foundational concepts that are essential to mastering the challenge of *Strategic Investing After 50:*

1. *Use of assets* (Chapter 4). Different assets may be used to accomplish different results. You need to understand what different instruments of the markets can be expected to do for you, and at what level of risk, before you can structure a portfolio correctly.

2. *Goals* (Chapter 5). Personal objectives drive the portfolio. To structure an appropriate portfolio, an investor needs to start with a clear enunciation of personal investment objectives for today and for tomorrow.

3. *Cash-flow analysis to help structure a demands-based portfolio* (Chapters 6 and 7). These are key chapters to read if you need to live off your portfolio. A simple cash-flow analysis will help you figure your needs. Then, you can structure your portfolio

based on those demands. This will help you allocate the correct percentage to bonds versus stocks in an income-producing portfolio.

4. *Strategy* (Chapter 8). The secret to success is to follow the three stages of personal portfolio management: accumulation, rebalancing, income production. This strategy works over a lifetime and takes the guesswork out of investment decisions.

5. *Tracking results* (Chapter 9)   Investing is not a competitive sport. The key is to monitor results against personal goals, in the context of what the markets can reasonably provide.

6. *Risk* (Chapter 10). Risk comes in many forms, one of which is of particular concern after 50. Not understanding what you are buying and how much you can lose is a particular problem for people who might be investing large sums of money for the first time in their lives. In discussing risk, I share a proprietary measure I use in my personal money management practice. Called "downside exposure," it is a way to measure the risk level you are assuming in your portfolio.

7. *Managing your personal portfolio* (Chapter 11). At this point in life, you need to take an overall view of your entire financial situation. Managing a portfolio is a new skill for many people who need to invest at this time of life.

8. *How to choose appropriate tools, including selection criteria and selling rules.* Investing for growth (Chapters 12 through 15); investing for income (Chapter 16); and investing for preservation of capital (Chapter 17).

9. *Using advisers wisely* (Chapter 18 and 19).

10. *Understanding your brokerage account* (Chapters 20 through 24). This section of the book deals with brokerage account management, from opening an account to working with your broker, and includes how to alert yourself to problems and how to get help to solve them.

Learning to navigate these foundational issues is a big step toward achieving the skills necessary to manage your own portfolio, either on your own or with an adviser.

Beyond these foundational lessons are special situations that you may encounter at this time of life: investment sales practices, fear-based products, and special trusts and estates and tax and distribution planning issues. I share with you some essential keys to help you avoid being lured into something you don't need and help you assess the best avenues for achieving what you do need as you move into the future. In the Appendix, I provide resources for further education and study.

No book can capture all you need to know about investing and relay it in such a way that you become expert at the task simply by reading. There are many limitations, not the least of which are the multivariate influences on the markets and the very personal nature of putting together a portfolio customized to meet that individual's particular needs. Given these circumstances, my goal is to give you some things to think about, direct you to some resources, and encourage you to continue learning strategic investing, which has come to be an essential life-skill of the twenty-first century. I wish you great success on your journey.

Julie Jason

Acknowledgments

For their kind assistance in dealing with some of the more complex tax and distribution issues covered in the book, special thanks are due to Manny Bernardo, former head of Deloitte & Touche, LLP, Connecticut Compensation and Benefits Tax Practice; Ed Slott, CPA, publisher of *Ed Slott's IRA Advisor*, Rockville Centre, New York; Jack E. Stephens, JD, LLM, author of *Avoiding the Tax Traps in Your IRA* (Fulton, TX: Legal Action Publication, 1999); Twila Slesnick, PhD, and John C. Suttle, JD, CPA, coauthors of *IRAs, 401(k)s & Other Retirement Plans: Taking Your Money Out* (Berkeley, CA: Nolo, 2000).

I thank Demetria and Janella Joyner and Cherise Wright for their solid support during the writing process and especially Johanna Lester for her dedication, loyalty, and effort, which is very much appreciated. I also thank my daughter, Ilona, for her moral support and encouragement (she liked the book), and my daughter, Leila, for clarifying the murky (she's the critic in the family).

A special thank you to my agent, Linda Mead, whose effectiveness, charm, and skill are unsurpassed, and my editors at John Wiley & Sons, Bob Shuman and David Pugh, who made this project a joy. And last but definitely not least, thanks to my clients, particularly those who took the time to read the manuscript and guide my hand, a hearty thank you.

J.J.

CHAPTER 1

The Difference 50 Makes

Age 50 is a turning point. And, it is a time of opportunity. If you approach it with some thought and preparation, you can begin a journey toward lifelong financial security. You still have the chance to build your portfolio to a sufficient size if you haven't done so. If you have, you can take steps to protect those assets and turn them into a stream of income for retirement.

Age 50 is also a time of consequences. At this age, actions have greater impact. A 30-year-old who loses 85 percent of his $1,000 investment in technology stocks can replace those assets much more easily than the 75-year-old who places the same trades and loses $850,000 of his $1 million retirement fund. Investable sums tend to be larger after 50. Losses hurt more. Money lost cannot be replaced in the same way it was acquired. This realization alone can help give you invaluable insight as to how to approach your own investment decisions from this point forward.

Irreplaceable Assets

If you saved all your working career and chose an investment strategy that lost you a significant amount, how would you replace it at the age of 70? Would you go back to work? If it took you 20 years to accumulate those assets, how long would it take you to replace the amount you lost? When considering your personal situation, you may find it helpful to think of your assets in terms of how easily you could *replace* them if necessary.

> **TIP**
>
> **When considering your personal situation, you may find it helpful to think of your assets in terms of how easily you could replace them if necessary.**

The same is true for assets you might acquire through an inheritance, buyout, divorce or legal settlement, pension distribution, sale of a home, sale of a business, or an insurance death benefit. If you lost a substantial part of this money, would you be able to replace it in the same manner? Usually the answer is no.

It helps to think of lifelong savings and assets acquired through once-in-a-lifetime events as "irreplaceable," since that gives them a certain importance that distinguishes the type of investing that you might have done at a younger age. *Irreplaceable assets* is a term I use to distinguish investments made from current earnings. Irreplaceable assets must be invested with more care, no matter the dollar amount involved. ***At this point in life, the problem investors need to solve is not how to make money, but how to make it last. At this point, there is less margin for error.***

Goals

Goals may also be different at this stage of life. A young person normally supports himself* through current earnings and invests for growth. These days, a retired individual will probably need to support himself with his own private savings, at least in part. At some point after 50, your portfolio may need to be structured to produce cash flow for living expenses.

---

* *Note:* The masculine pronoun refers to both masculine and feminine.

Risk

In some cases, a person over 50 may take on more risk than is prudent, probably because he did not build sufficient assets when young. A younger investor will be more focused on compounding to help build assets over time. Due to a shorter investment horizon, an older individual cannot expect to see the multiplier factor create as much wealth as he would like.

NOTE

Compounding is the mathematical phenomenon that affects rates of growth of an investment over time. It is the multiplier effect.

Changes in Pension Expectations

Before retirement, your living expenses are covered by your paycheck. Not too long ago, workers could expect their pension to support them through retirement. When added to Social Security retirement benefits, such pensions generally covered the lifelong expenses of long-term employees.

That was yesterday. Today, there are four strong reasons why this is no longer economic reality:

1. People are living much longer than 68 or 70, the life span of a working male just a few years ago.

2. People change jobs much more frequently and do not qualify for lifelong pensions of any significance.

3. Fewer companies offer lifelong pensions.

4. Social Security benefits may not be meaningful. The maximum annual benefit you will receive from Social Security usually pays for only a fraction of your living expenses.

CAUTION

Realistically, today, an individual must look to himself as the primary source of retirement income.

Realistically, today, an individual must look to himself as the primary source of retirement income.

Strategy

While it is always important to invest against a plan, strategy becomes even more important after 50. A 30-year-old may get away with occasional stock picking without a plan. But, at 50 and beyond, random activity will not be very productive. At this stage in life, it helps to have a good strategy that takes into account your particular situation based on your particular needs in retirement.

Tracking Results

Monitoring your progress also takes on more importance after 50. Many investors go through life without knowing whether they are saving enough for retirement. Part of the problem is that they have not discovered a way to monitor their results. At this time in life, you need to monitor against your own personal goals, instead of arbitrary benchmarks set by common wisdom.

NOTE

A benchmark is a standard used to evaluate the performance of investment. A common benchmark for stock performance is the S&P 500 index.

Regular monitoring against personal goals helps assure that you are making the right investment decisions. Monitoring is also important for another reason. Reviewing your results regularly gives you a chance to correct an error or a bad decision if you need to do so, before getting too far afield. At this point in life, you need to limit mistakes to a minimum, by catching them before they cause irreparable damage.

Summary

Today, you need to look to your own assets as a source of financial stability going forward into the future. In some cases, you may need to pay for a good part of your own living expenses with the money you saved throughout your life. Many people who are entering their 50s have been saving money through their company savings plans, Individual Retirement Accounts (IRAs), and personal investment accounts. Lawyers, doctors, businesspeople, nurses, teachers, and social workers, alike, often have accumulated sizable sums of money for retirement. Acquiring or having significant savings does not mean you have the wherewithal to know what to do with it.

In Chapter 2, let's take a look at common misperceptions about the financial markets and then in Chapter 3, let's consider what you can reasonably expect to achieve with your own investments.

Common Misconceptions about the Market That Might Affect Your Decisions

Three misconceptions about the market need to be put to rest: the new economy, market timing, and concentration.

The New Economy: A Magic Carpet Ride

In January 2000, a conservative 70-year-old gentleman with a balanced portfolio asked me if he should sell everything and buy Internet stocks. At the time, returns for the highest flying stocks and mutual funds were dazzling everyone. The question I posed was, "What about risk?"

"This market is different," Jim replied. "Technology and Internet stocks will continue to go up, even if they are costly to buy. Things have changed and I don't want to be left behind."

Ah, yes, the new economy, the new rules, the new paradigm. When a normally conservative person buys into the current fad, it is a sign of the end of a speculative market. The incident made me think of Wall Street financier, Bernard Baruch, who, the story goes, sold all his stocks just before the great crash of 1929, when his shoeshine boy offered him a stock tip. The 1999–2000 technology bubble burst a few months after Jim's visit and he was indeed happy that he had not thrown caution to the wind.

History teaches us that major technological advances fueled speculative fervor in the past and that we should expect the same in future markets. In the 1920s, the automobile and the radio were the technological wonders of the time, both of which still play a major role in our lives. It took 35 years, however, for Radio Corporation of America (RCA) to recover its 1929 price peak.

The same was true of the late 1960s bull market. Dominated by the "Nifty Fifty," the Standard and Poor's (S&P) 500 Index was driven by consumer goods and technology stocks. However, higher inflation, monetary tightening, and cheaper imports from Japan led to two bear markets—first in 1969–1970 and again in 1973–1974. During the latter period, stock market averages dropped about 50 percent. Many of the Nifty Fifty dropped by as much 80 percent to 90 percent, some reaching their ultimate lows in 1977 and 1978.

> **NOTE**
>
> In the 1960s, the stocks of 50 well-known companies called the "Nifty Fifty" dominated the stock market.

In these declines, an important factor was the Federal Reserve Bank's shift to a more restrictive monetary policy by raising interest rates and decreasing money supply. But in early 2000, the Fed was sending mixed signals by increasing interest rates and increasing, not decreasing, money supply in response to Y2K worries. Some believe that this increased money supply fueled the Nasdaq market and the speculative bubble in technology stocks. In addition, true believers argued that record-setting business expansion distinguished prior periods of stock market fever. But in fact, past business expansion cycles actually have been greater.

> **NOTE**
>
> The Nasdaq stock market lists nearly 5,000 companies and is a subsidiary of the National Association of Securities Dealers, Inc. (NASD).

Highly speculative bull markets such as the technology market of late 1999 and early 2000 create a careless attitude on the part of investors who, inspired by wishful thinking and the stories of fortunes being made by others, close their eyes to risk. Based on the belief that they are being left behind in a market that will not go down, they gleefully abandon their normal caution. Sadly, many who entered the fray at fever pitch are still not facing the facts.

Market Timing

The stock market is a mystery to many who try to predict its movements. Attempting to predict the market is as fruitless as attempting to change base metals into gold (alchemy was a legitimate profession in 1500). Today, market timers seem to be trying to perfect that craft. Can anyone name a professional money manager or individual investor who has successfully made and acted on his predictions over any length of time? If there were such a person, he would be famous. But there is no such person or program; predictions do not work for any length of time in different types of markets.

Publishers of market timing services take a different view. Some of these services may be helpful from time to time to confirm your assumptions about the direction of the market, or to follow a trading pattern that may turn out to be profitable. However, I have not seen a timing service that is helpful to the average investor. Assessing a program and its predictive ability in all types of markets is a hard, if not impossible, task for an individual to undertake.

But, do you have to try to predict the market? That depends on what kind of investor you are. If you are buying a stock to make money on a short-term trade, you are taking that bet based on a strong conviction that the stock is going up. Therefore, you are predicting that move, and you either have a crystal ball or some convincing reason to support that conviction.

NOTE

When you sell short, you are hoping the stock will go down in price.

You simply do not invest in a stock if you think the stock is going down, unless you are selling short. If you are trading, you need to have a workable predictive model for both the stock and the market. I discuss this in greater detail in Chapter 11.

Not all situations call for predictions about the future. A long-term investor who diversifies across several sectors does not need a crystal ball, because the market has an upward bias. Long-term investors will participate in the growth of the market over time, as long as they don't panic and sell in a downturn. As you can see, your job as a long-term investor is very different from that of a short-term investor.

Concentration

As online trading and television financial news programs began to affect individual investor behavior, we started seeing a move away from diversification to concentration. Concentration involves buying a single stock or a single sector. Diversification involves buying multiple stocks and sectors.

Concentration is favored by momentum stock traders who wish to make large and quick profits in an upwardly trending market. Success in late 1999 and early 2000 gave many people the false notion that they were good at picking winners. But the fact of the matter is that investment genius is *trend dependent.* Individuals were pulled along with the bull market. As Warren Buffett said in Berkshire Hathaway's 1996 annual report, referring to its 1995 performance, "This is a year in which any fool could make a bundle in the stock market. As we did. To paraphrase President Kennedy, a rising tide lifts all yachts."

NOTE

Concentration involves buying a single stock or a single sector. Diversification involves buying multiple stocks and sectors.

Ranking at the top of the technology sector for January and February 2000, an electrical equipment manufacturer started out the year at $5 a share and hit a high of $98 by the end of February. Speculators who bought in January made an incredible profit of over 1,000 percent. As an individual investor, you might have discovered the stock in February. If you had bought it at the time, you would have suffered a loss of 50 percent in just a few weeks.

Concentration is a current fad. It is a great concept. But, it is one of those ideas that is simple to understand and difficult to execute. Most people enter the game much too late to find winners. And among those who get lucky early, many cannot repeat the exercise.

Diversification

Diversification is not a fad. In fact, some would say diversification is old-fashioned, since diversification makes your returns average. Diversified stock portfolios tend to produce average returns. Over the past 10 years average returns meant 17 percent per year, which is the average annual return on the broad market as measured by the S&P 500 Index ending December 2000. Moreover, diversification will help you make more money in the long run by protecting you against severe losses. A diversified portfolio is less risky than a concentrated portfolio, which over time, translates into higher returns. Why? For the simple reason that it is extremely important to know when to cut your losses in a concentrated portfolio, and this is something that most people do not know how to do.

Summary

Before beginning an investment program, it is helpful to understand some of the common misconceptions about how to invest in the market, since they can influence your behavior. At some time in the future, someone may tell you that we are working with new rules in the stock market. Anytime you hear that, you can bet that we are in a speculative market fueled by people who do not remember the last bubble before it burst.

Before you are enticed to purchase or be swayed by a market timing system that will predict the market for you, remember that if Nobel Prize winning economists cannot come up with one that works for any length of time, do you really think you can? If you are thinking of taking all your hard-earned assets and buying one or two stocks that have no place to go but up, remember that concentration works only if you were born under a lucky star and have an iron-clad selling discipline.

TIP

Diversification will help you make money in the long run by lessening the severe losses you might experience if you concentrate your investments in a few stocks or industries that fall into disfavor.

CHAPTER 3

Reasonable Expectations

When reading this chapter, keep in mind that some of the terms used here are not defined because they are discussed in detail in later chapters.

When a stockbroker suggests a stock, your expectation is that the stock will go up after you buy it. Unless you are selling short, you are working with the assumption that you will be able to sell the stock for a profit, hopefully sizable, some day in the future.

To the uninitiated, unspoken promises of profits form the basis of a decision to buy. But the fact of the matter is that innumerable influences affect the price of a stock and not all stock picks will result in profitable trades. It is unreasonable to expect that you will make a profit on every stock that you buy. The success of an individual trade will depend on the continued accuracy of your assumptions, the time you give to the effort, the skill with which you execute the strategy, and the many influences on the stock itself and the market as a whole, many of which cannot be predicted or known with any degree of certainty.

What Are Reasonable Expectations?

It is reasonable to expect that some trades will result in losses, no matter how skilled you are as an investor. With losing trades, success is measured by how skillfully you can keep your losses to a manageable overall level.

In fact, taking losses is one of the most important lessons an investor over 50 has to learn. In Chapter 14, we'll discuss how to set up your own selling rules so that you can protect yourself before losses become irrecoverable. We'll also discuss how to select stocks and stock mutual funds in Chapters 13 and 15.

What is a reasonable expectation for returns on an overall portfolio? All things considered, if you have a growth objective and you approach your stock investing with caution, you can reasonably expect a sound diversified stock portfolio to double every 6 to 12 years or so, depending on the state of the market. Given historical perspective, you can also expect that the market value of your well-selected diversified stock portfolio could drop 20 percent or more in any given year. You would expect similar results from well-chosen diversified large company stock mutual funds. At the end of this chapter, I provide supporting statistics behind these conclusions and discuss how to interpret this data.

On the other hand, if you concentrate your portfolio or use leverage to improve your chances of a big hit, you may double your investment within a matter of weeks or months, given the right environment. As many people saw in 1999 and early 2000, just about anyone who bought technology stocks rode the profit wave in a big way. On the other side of the coin are the huge losses that resulted when the wave crashed, particularly when leverage was involved. Your potential losses could be as high as 95 percent without leverage. With leverage, you might be asked to sell your home to pay off the money the broker lent you for margin. We will discuss leverage and margin more fully in Chapter 23.

In the bond market, it is reasonable to expect annual interest payments ranging between 5 and 10 percent, with the lower range representing the highest quality paper and the higher range representing high-risk debt (discussed in Chapter 16). At the same time, you have to factor in the expectation of market fluctuation the longer the maturity. Even the most creditworthy paper fluctuates in market price in changing interest rate environments. Although U.S. Treasury bonds are the most creditworthy debt obligations you can buy, you will lose money if you have to sell them before maturity in a rising-interest-rate scenario. Let's say you bought 30-year U.S. Treasury bonds on February 15, 1977, yielding 7⅝ percent and maturing on February 15, 2007. If you found yourself in an emergency situation and had to sell the bonds in May 1984, you would receive far less than you paid for them. You see, in 1984, an investor could have bought 30-year U.S. Treasury bonds yielding 13.25 percent, almost twice as much as your bonds. Since bonds are an important part of an income investor's portfolio, I discuss how bond pricing works in detail in Chapter 16.

In the money markets, you can reasonably expect a short-term rate of return of about 4 percent to 5 percent, with hardly any principal exposure. By definition, money market instruments are short-term in nature, thus eliminating some of the worries of changes in interest rates. Quality can be an issue, however, and needs to be checked and understood. Poor credit quality would increase the risk of default. Chapter 17 covers more on money market investing.

NOTE

When you use leverage, you are investing with borrowed money. Margin is a form of leverage in which you are borrowing from your brokerage firm.

Inflation also needs to be considered because your return will be less in real terms if you discount your dollars to account for loss of purchasing power. Stocks of large companies as represented by the S&P 500 Index, returned 11.3 percent per year before inflation for the period 1929 through 1999, and 8 percent compound annual returns in real terms (inflation-adjusted), according to Ibbotson Associates. Over the same period, Ibbotson reports that corporate bonds returned 5.6 percent compounded annually on a nominal basis and 2.5 percent in real, inflation-adjusted terms. Long-term government bonds returned 5.1 percent nominally and 2.0 percent after inflation. Treasury bills returned 3.8 percent before inflation and 0.7 percent after inflation.

The effects of inflation indicate that of the asset classes considered, Treasury bills would have beaten inflation by a hair, U.S. government bonds by 2.0 percent, corporate bonds by 2.5 percent, and large company stocks by 8 percent.

What you can reasonably expect in your own situation will be a reflection of past markets, tempered by how you approach investing. If you take a devil-may-care attitude, you can expect some dramatic gains if you are lucky, probably followed by some sad and possibly severe losses—hopefully the kind from which recovery is possible. If you approach investing with thought and reason, you can expect to achieve positive results over time with interim losses from time to time. Whether you can meet your personal goals, assuming you have defined them with care and due consideration, will depend more on your approach and less on luck than you might think.

When considering expectations, a common problem occurs in interpreting the data previously discussed. If you are a student of the market, you are familiar with Ibbotson Associates, the research house in Chicago referred to earlier as the source of market data and analysis dating back to 1926.

Ibbotson also is the source of the often quoted 10 percent return expectation for the broad market. Over time, according to Ibbotson, the broad market, as measured by the S&P 500 Index, averaged an annual return of 10 percent with a standard deviation of 20 percent (*Stocks, Bonds, Bills, and Inflation 1993 Yearbook*, Ibbotson Associates). Updated through 1999, the average annual return is reported at 11.3 percent return with a standard deviation of 20.1 percent (*Stocks, Bonds, Bills, and Inflation 2000 Yearbook*, Ibbotson Associates).

> **TIP**
>
> Whether you will meet your personal goals, assuming you have defined them with care and due consideration, will depend more on your approach and less on luck than you might think.

Let's use the 10 percent return, and see how that estimate is often misinterpreted, even by attorneys, accountants, the financial press, and financial advisers. The following example illustrates the problem.

At 63, Joe is in good health and wants to retire early. Over his working career, he has saved $1 million. He needs $100,000 a year for living expenses above what he expects to get from Social Security and he does not want to change his life style.

Given the 10 percent return expectation on large capitalization stocks, you would expect that Joe would be all set. With $1 million in assets, $100,000 a year is exactly the 10 percent return he needs. But, let's go a little deeper. There are two problems with using this 10 percent return to calculate expected income of $100,000 on a $1 million portfolio, even ignoring the tax and inflation concerns for the moment.

First, the 10 percent figure is not income, it is total return. Total return is the sum of two numbers, growth and income. The 10 percent return is a sum of 6 percent growth and 4 percent income, according to Ibbotson. Second, the 10 percent expectation is a return averaged over a long time that includes periods of higher returns as well as lower or negative returns.

Let's say Joe, age 63, invested his entire $1 million in a hypothetical S&P 500 index investment in 1975. Not only would Joe be able to take out $100,000 a year partly from income and partly from principal, he would also have millions left over for his children to inherit.

> **▼ NOTE**
>
> **Total return is the sum of two numbers, growth and income.**

But if Joe had started in 1973 instead, in just two years his $1 million account would have dropped by more than one-half to $470,000, due to a market loss of 14 percent in 1973, followed by a loss of 20 percent in 1974. Joe would be completely out of money before the age of 73.

Stock market averages need to be understood for what they are. Total return cannot be treated as an income distribution. A large component of total return is price appreciation (and depreciation). As you plan for the future, remember to gauge down market expectations before committing to long-term actions.

> **▼ CAUTION**
>
> **The often quoted "10 percent return expectation" for the broad market, as measured by the S&P 500 Index, is a reflection of two numbers. Capital appreciation represents 6 percent. The remainder is a dividend reinvestment of 4 percent.**

Summary

An individual over 50 who is investing irreplaceable assets needs to have a good understanding of what to expect from his investments. Historical market data is available to help you put expectations into a realistic framework. Working outside of that framework is possible—you can increase potential reward by concentrating on leverage, but by doing so, you increase the probability of losses. Expecting too much leads to trouble.

CHAPTER 4

The Appropriate Use of Assets

You could try to use *any* instrument of the market to try to grow a nest egg in preparation for retirement or to create monthly cash flow after retirement to replace your salary. Some will be more effective than others. In this chapter, I introduce a concept I call *appropriate use of assets*, which is one of the basic building concepts that people tend to miss when they start to invest. If you understand the uses of assets, you can make some sound judgments about the best types of investments for your portfolio, a subject developed over the next six chapters.

Using Assets Appropriately

Just as there are appropriate uses for ordinary tools such as hammers, can openers, and tire jacks, there are appropriate uses for assets. When you want to hang a picture, you probably pick up a hammer to pound the nail into the wall.

If you had never seen a hammer and only had a can opener, you might not know that a hammer is a more effective tool for securing a nail into the wall. You could try using the can opener instead, but the task would probably be difficult. Hammering is simply not the usage intended by the manufacturer of the can opener.

Similarly, if you have never seen a bond ladder spinning off monthly cash flows you can spend in retirement, you may not realize growth stocks are far less effective for this purpose. Individual growth stocks may not pay dividends and can be quite volatile. In a sense, the "manufacturer" never intended growth stocks to be used for income production.

TIP

You could try to use any instrument of the market to try to grow a nest egg in preparation for retirement or to create monthly cash flow after retirement to replace your salary. Some will be more effective than others.

There are more appropriate and less appropriate uses for financial assets, all of which depend on what you are trying to achieve. Each goal should be dealt with separately. Unless you are vying for recognition in *Ripley's Believe It or Not*, you would not want to try to hammer a nail into the wall while opening a can and changing a tire. Likewise, you don't want to juggle assets to produce different goals. Instead, it's best to divide your portfolio into components, one for each purpose you are trying to achieve.

If you strip away all the glitter and look at an investment possibility dispassionately, you will find that there are three essential uses to which you can put your assets: (1) A single dollar can be put to work for growth (capital appreciation), (2) to produce cash flow (production of income), or (3) for safety (preservation of capital). All the possible investments you can make for your core portfolio fall into one or a combination of these three uses. Ancillary uses such as hedging, writing options, leveraging, short selling, and trading are all subordinate to these three primary uses. In each case, you are giving your assets to someone for a specific purpose and with a specific expectation.

TIP

You can create a bond ladder by buying a number of bonds with sequential maturities; for example, bond 1 matures in 2005, bond 2 matures in 2006, and so on. This helps you diversify against interest rate risk.

Capital Appreciation

When you invest for capital appreciation, the underlying assumption is that you will buy an investment today with the expectation that you will get back a larger amount at some future date when you sell it. To achieve capital appreciation, or growth, you need to buy the tools of the marketplace designed for that purpose. Individual stocks serve this goal (discussed in Chapters 12, 13, and 14), as do instruments that package stocks, such as stock mutual funds (discussed in detail in Chapter 15), stock unit trusts, or exchange traded stock funds such as "iShares." A stock unit trust is an investment company that purchases a fixed portfolio of stocks. Exchange traded funds are index funds that are traded just like stocks.

Most people are aware that no promises are attached to common stocks by the corporations that issue them. Stocks are not guaranteed by anyone to grow your assets. Companies that declare and pay dividends on their common stocks actually have no legal obligation to do so. Instead of promises, guarantees, or contractual responsibilities, the investor makes do with the underlying hope and expectation that he will sell the stock to someone else at a higher price than his purchase price.

> **NOTE**
>
> There are three essential uses to which you can put your assets. A single dollar can be put to work (1) for growth (capital appreciation), (2) to produce cash flow (production of income), or (3) for safety (preservation of capital).

Production of Income

Let's say you have been investing in stocks for the length of your working career and now are retired and need $5,000 a month to pay for living expenses. You can try to do this by selling stocks out of your portfolio each month as you need money. What do you do if some of your stocks drop dramatically in price, as many stocks do from time to time? Do you stop paying your bills? Imagine trying to determine which stocks you should sell each month under those circumstances.

The premise here is that, whenever possible, income should generally be derived from income-producing investments, instead of from capital raised by selling off principal. It is better to use the instruments of the market that are intended to produce cash flow, those offering interest or dividend distributions. As mentioned, some stocks and stock mutual funds pay dividends, which are a form of cash flow that you can spend for living expenses. Bonds pay interest and bond mutual funds pay dividends, both of which you can also spend

> **NOTE**
>
> iShares, distributed by SEI Investments Distribution Co., are examples of exchange traded funds. Each share represents a portfolio of stocks designed to closely track a specific stock index. iShares are like stocks in that you can buy and sell them the same way you would buy and sell the stock of an individual company.

when you need your portfolio to produce cash for you. For cash flow purposes, bonds and other fixed income instruments of the market are a better choice than stocks. First, bonds will tend to pay higher distributions than stocks. Second, bond distributions for a particular bond are generally fixed in amount; stock distributions are not. Third, bond distributions are set for a period of time (until the maturity date of the bond), offering the opportunity for better planning.

As discussed in Chapter 16, bonds generally promise two things, return of principal at some particular future date when the bond matures or expires, and interest payments from the date of issue until maturity. The issuer of the bond generally guarantees neither the repayment of principal nor interest payments. Both will depend on whether the issuer can stay in business. If the issuer does close its doors, as did International Harvester, and numerous other bankrupt companies, the bondholder can lose both the income stream and, in the worst case, all the principal. Municipalities issuing bonds can also go out of business; this almost happened to New York City, which found itself on the brink of bankruptcy in the mid-1970s.

> **TIP**
>
> You can either reinvest your mutual fund dividends to purchase additional shares of the fund or have the dividends paid to you in cash.

Preservation of Capital and Stability of Principal

Sometimes, you want your money to be safe above all else. With money market instruments, your assumption is that you will receive your original investment back and no less, plus interest. The best financial tools to achieve stability of principal are short-term money market instruments, such as U.S. Treasury bills, certificates of deposit, and money market mutual funds. Money market instruments are discussed in Chapter 17.

Summary

Different instruments of the market, such as stocks, bonds, and Treasury bills, have different purposes. One of the paths to becoming a successful investor after 50 is to see how they differ so you can use them for your own needs. Portfolio objectives are the subject of Chapter 5.

Understanding Portfolio Objectives

Of all the factors involved in structuring a sound portfolio after 50, none is more important than setting investment objectives because they shape your investment decisions and determine your results. If you haven't given your investment objectives much thought, you might be working with an unstated—and perhaps unmanageable—goal such as "My objective is to make as much money as possible as quickly as possible."

While this might be a valid objective for a speculative trader, you need to think long and hard before making it your goal because it can lead you to take on some very big risks and make you easy prey for the unscrupulous.

In this chapter, let's discuss setting investment objectives based on the following uses of assets: growing your capital, paying you income, and preserving your capital. Here we talk about general concepts. Then, in Chapters 6, 7, and 8, I introduce the concept of setting objectives based on the demands of the portfolio, which is a way to structure your portfolio so that you can pay yourself a stream of income throughout retirement.

Let's zero in on your current and primary investment objectives. By *primary objective*, I mean the objective to which you assign the highest priority. The *secondary objective* takes a backseat to the primary objective. Let's look at three examples.

Question 1. Let's say you are 50 and employed full time. All your expenses are covered by your paycheck, and you have money left over to invest. Should you be investing for growth, income, or stability of principal?

Answer 1. Your primary objective will be growth, and you will be investing in instruments of the market that offer growth of capital, such as stocks or stock mutual funds. Depending on other holdings and circumstances, you may have a secondary objective of income or preservation of capital to diversify your holdings across asset classes.

> **CAUTION**
> If you haven't given your investment objectives much thought, you might be working with an unstated goal such as "My objective is to make as much money as possible as quickly as possible."

Question 2. You are 77 years old, and you are no longer working. Your Social Security covers one half of what you need to live on and you have $500,000 in liquid assets. In such a financial situation, should you be investing for growth, income, or stability of principal?

Answer 2. Your primary objective will be income production since you need to generate cash flow for living expenses. To accomplish this, you will be investing in instruments that produce income, such as bonds or bond funds. You may also need to continue to build capital by investing in stocks, and as a result, your secondary objective would be growth. And, you may wish to use part of your portfolio for preservation of capital by investing in short-term money market instruments, such as Treasury bills. Since investing for income will be an objective for most people over 50 at some time in their lives, you'll need to know how much of your portfolio to allocate to the primary objective based on your personal situation. The percentage will be based on the demands you will be placing on the portfolio, as explained in Chapter 6. Of all the objectives, this is probably most important to plan.

Question 3. Never married, you are 65 and have a lifelong pension that not only fully covers all your needs, but also increases yearly to cover future needs by offsetting inflation. You have no investment experience. You have just come into a large inheritance that you do not want to jeopardize under any circumstances. Should you invest for growth, income, or preservation of capital?

Answer 3. Preservation of capital may be your primary objective for your inheritance. By investing in instruments intended for preservation of capital, such as U.S. Treasury bills, you will be able to protect your inheritance from serious losses. You may also have a secondary objective of diversification with fixed income by buying some bonds.

By tying your own investment objectives to use of assets, you can invest in stocks for growth, bonds for income, and money market instruments for preservation of capital. Some people actually have all three objectives at work at the same time. If you do, you want to split your portfolio into parts that you use for each of the different objectives. You can have a portion that produces income. Another portion is invested for growth. A third portion is invested for preservation of capital to stabilize your portfolio and protect your principal. As the concepts developed in the next two chapters indicate, how much money you use for each purpose will turn on demands you place on your overall portfolio. The biggest demands for investors after 50 will be the need for regular cash flow as well as continued growth.

> **NOTE**
> By primary objective, I mean the objective that you give the highest priority. The secondary objective takes a backseat to the primary objective.

Other Objectives

The three objectives that we have been discussing are the basics. There are many variations on the theme. Most brokerage account forms list several growth objectives, including aggressive growth and speculation. It is important to know how to relate your objectives to a stockbroker if you intend to work with one. In Chapter 21, we'll review some of the issues involved in dealing with brokerage account investment objectives.

Primary versus Secondary Objective Illustrated

Should you always have a secondary objective? The following situation illustrates when you may not. Say your retirement portfolio is not as large as you would like, you have no need for current income, and you are used to investing through monthly payroll deductions. This was the situation with Janice, a reader of my weekly financial column. At age 54, single, and employed with a large company, Janice was 100 percent invested in stock mutual funds through her company 401(k) plan. She planned to work until age 65. She had no pension benefit coming to her and her 401(k) was her only asset. She was used to investing in the stock market and was not concerned about market fluctuations. She had enough money in a bank account to cover 6 months of expenses in an emergency. She lived modestly and had money left over after expenses each month, which she put in a bank account. This is a perfect example of a situation calling for a primary growth objective and no secondary objective. Investing 100 percent of her 401(k) contributions entirely for growth for now was quite reasonable in the circumstances. As Janice gets closer to retirement, however, she will have to reconsider her objectives and possibly switch to a primary objective of income. As described in Chapters 6 and 7, there is a way to calculate how much Janice will need to set aside for income production when that becomes her primary objective after retirement.

Stocks versus Bonds

If you have not been investing enough and now find yourself trying to catch up, how do you determine if you should invest only for growth? Whether you should add a secondary objective of income or preservation of capital will depend on these factors: your experience as an investor, whether you have a pension or other sources of retirement income, and how much time is left before retirement. None of these factors alone is determinative. You need to weigh all of them.

Experience

If you are an inexperienced investor, limiting yourself to stocks or stock mutual funds alone may be too risky. You may need to add a secondary objective of income for diversification through bonds. Generally—but not always—the volatility of your portfolio will decrease with the addition of bonds and money market funds. You may have 60 percent stocks and 40 percent bonds, instead of 100 percent in stocks. Or for even more safety, you may put 50 percent toward growth, with a secondary objective of preservation of capital for the remainder. In either case, if you need to grow your capital, your primary objective needs to be growth.

Pension

If you have a lifelong pension coming to you that will cover your expenses in retirement, you may not have a growth objective at all. Perhaps you want safety above all else, in which case you will have a primary objective of preservation of capital. If you do want growth to leave money to your children, you might want to temper it by having a primary objective of growth and a secondary objective of income or preservation of capital. You could have 60 percent in growth and 40 percent in income or preservation of capital.

Time Horizon

The more time you have until retirement, the more time you have for compounding to work in your favor. A long horizon gives you a chance to ride through just about any underperforming period in the stock market and would support the argument for you not to dilute your growth objective by adding bonds. If you have 10 years or more on your side, you can be 100 percent invested in the stock market. You need some flexibility in terms

> **NOTE**
> Compounding is the mathematical phenomenon that affects rates of growth of an investment over time. It is the multiplier effect.

of how and when you will be converting those assets to income, however. You do not want to find yourself needing to cash in a stock portfolio in a down market. Someone with a shorter horizon may wish—and have a strong rationale—to invest a portion of his portfolio in bonds and money markets.

Summary

There are many personal factors to consider before deciding on stock and bond allocations. Most people can follow these general rules. Invest in stocks for growth when you need to grow your assets, but be ready to ride out the fluctuations of the market. Invest in bonds for income when you need money to live on or for diversification. Invest in money markets to stabilize a portfolio at any age. If your one and only objective is growth, add bonds or money markets if you want to lessen the risk of a 100 percent stock portfolio.

In the next chapter, you will learn how to compute your retirement income gap, which will bring you closer to understanding how to set your own objectives when you need to create cash flow in retirement, and in Chapter 7, I'll show you how a couple actually applied these concepts in their own portfolios.

CHAPTER 6

Understanding Capital Commitment Based on Cash-Flow Demands

In this chapter, we will be tackling the question of how to set up your portfolio to generate cash that you can spend. We will consider how to figure the amount you need from your portfolio at different times of life, including retirement, as well as how to structure your portfolio to produce the cash flow you need. Some readers will be able to do the calculations provided in this chapter on their own. Others may want to seek out the assistance of an appropriate adviser. This discussion shows you a workable but simplified version of the process of structuring a portfolio based on the premise that income should be derived from income-producing investments. (For those who believe stocks should be sold for cash flow purposes, a concept discussed in Chapter 4.) *Note that for simplicity the discussion that follows does not show the impact of taxes, which also needs to be calculated before final allocations can be made.*

First, let me introduce you to a cash flow concept called the *retirement income gap*. This is a term used by company benefits specialists to indicate the gap between how much money an individual needs to live on and what he actually receives from his pension, Social Security, and other retirement plans.

You may also have a *current income gap*. A current income gap can hit you at any age, usually as a result of a change of circumstances, such as a divorce, death of a spouse, disability, or loss of a job. Many times, people who go through such life-changing events have a fear of facing their finances. But, facing the facts helps determine the gap and solve the problem. A specific example can illustrate these concepts.

A year after her divorce, Marge was not sure how much she was spending and she was afraid to find out. With some encouragement, she set up a system to track her spending over a three-month period, which might be helpful for you as well. Marge collected all her receipts and canceled checks for the previous three months. She placed them into three stacks, one for each of three categories: (1) absolute essentials and fixed costs, such as housing expenses and real estate taxes; (2) flexible essentials, such as clothing; (3) discretionary expenses, such as vacations or entertainment.

Calculating the Income Gap

After stacking up all the bills relating to housing, Marge realized she was using up all her income to pay only one expense category. Her entire $6,000 alimony check paid for the monthly cost of maintaining the large home the family had occupied before the divorce. There was nothing left over for category 2 and category 3 expenses. She was spending about $1,000 apiece for each, bringing her total expenses to $8,000 a month. This was an eye-opener: She was short $24,000 a year. With this knowledge, Marge could pinpoint her problem and solve it. Her housing costs were too high for her income. She could sell her home and scale down. Or, if she wanted to stay there, she could supplement her income by getting a job. Or, she could look to her other assets to generate additional monthly income.

Filling the Income Gap

After reviewing her spending, Marge knew she was short $24,000 a year. That was her current income gap. How could she use her $1 million divorce settlement to fill the income gap if she wanted to? Let's go through the calculations, which you can apply in your situation as well. You would use this basic set of calculations to figure out how to structure your portfolio if you had income production as an objective. Risk is an important part of the analysis.

Calculate Low-Risk Yields First

Always start with the safest of investments, a 3-month U.S. Treasury bill (see Chapter 17). For this illustration, let's assume a 5 percent yield.

Then, ask yourself how much of the $1 million principal you need to commit to produce $24,000, assuming you bought a Treasury bill yielding 5 percent. Remembering high school algebra, you find that $480,000 of capital invested at 5 percent gives you $24,000 of income before taxes. (Hint: Divide $24,000 by .05 to get $480,000.) The math tells you how much money you need to generate $24,000 a year before taxes if your investment pays you a cash flow of 5 percent.

> **TIP**
>
> If you have income production as an objective, structure your portfolio only after you know your income gap and capital commitment.

Next Compare High-Risk Yield

Now look at a high return, which is the opposite end of the risk-reward spectrum. Consider a high-risk high-yield bond (bonds are discussed in Chapter 16). In this illustration, use a 10 percent return. Using the same formula as above, you would need $240,000 of capital invested at 10 percent to yield $24,000 before taxes. (If you divide $24,000 by .10, you get $240,000.) You only need $240,000 of assets to free up $24,000 cash flow if your yield is 10 percent. As we saw above, you need $480,000 of capital when you are working with a 5 percent yield.

Capital Commitment

These two extremes give you a range of expectations of how much capital you need to commit to produce a certain amount of income. In this illustration, if you need to have additional pretax income of $24,000 a year, you can produce that by using capital of between $240,000 and $480,000, depending on the risk level you wish to assume. The less risk you are willing to assume, the more capital you will need.

Structuring the Portfolio

To finish off the example, let's say Marge chooses a mid-risk option, which will be a combination of higher quality and lower quality higher yielding bonds with a combined yield of 7.5 percent. That means the bond portion of her portfolio would be funded with $320,000 (using the previous calculation) to produce $24,000 before taxes, which is her primary investment objective.

> **NOTE**
>
> The less risk you are willing to assume, the more capital you will need.

Now she can figure her secondary objective, which is growth. Having $680,000 left, she could invest the full amount for growth and choose stocks and stock mutual funds. If she were risk averse, Marge could lower that amount to include an objective of preservation of capital. How much would go into each portion would depend on her personal preferences.

Retirement Expenses

I'm sure you see how this exercise relates to retirement income. You need to know how much you will be spending on living expenses each year during your retirement to see if you will need to supplement your Social Security and other pension benefits with your own investments. How do you figure future expenses? Start by adding up all your current expenses, except income taxes. If you fall within the norms published by the U.S. Department of Labor, you can expect that you will spend 30 percent less in the first year of retirement than you do your last year of work. For example, if you are 64 and spend $30,000 a year for living expenses, and don't plan on changing your lifestyle much after retirement, you can expect to spend $21,000 your first year of retirement.

This rule of thumb does not apply in all situations. For example, if you plan on traveling after you retire, you will need to increase your estimate accordingly. Also, the estimate is based on today's dollars. You will need to adjust it for year-to-year increases in the cost of living due to inflation, which can complicate matters when trying to do those calculations on your own. For a minimal assessment, you can do your calculations in today's dollars and ask yourself how much you would need in assets today to cover those needs using the concepts discussed in this chapter. (If you do not have those assets, then you need to start saving and investing more vigorously.) If you wish to calculate the assets you would need to have in future dollars and don't want to do the projections yourself, you may find a good retirement calculator online. Since inflation will be a factor to contend with, let's discuss that briefly.

Inflation

While our current inflation rate is lower, based on history, you can reasonably assume that inflation during your retirement will average somewhere between 3 percent and 6 percent per year.

Assuming 3 percent annual inflation through-out your retirement, if you are 65 today, by the time you are 89, your $21,000 would have one-half the buying power it does today. That is, at 89 you would need $42,000 to pay for the same expenses that cost $21,000 when you were 65. At 6 percent inflation, if you are 65 today, you will need $42,000 when you are 77 and $84,000 when you are 89.

TIP

To find out your own estimated Social Security benefits, call Social Security at 800-772-1213 and ask for your "Personal Earnings Statement and Estimate of Future Benefits."

Pension and Social Security Benefits

Next, figure out how much you will receive in annual pension and So-cial Security payments. Remember that while Social Security benefits are indexed to inflation, most pension benefits are not. Then you can see what you'll really be getting to help you calculate your retirement income gap. We will talk more about Social Security in Chapter 30.

The Demands-Based Formula

To see how much capital you need to generate a particular yearly cash flow at different interest rates, use the same formula discussed earlier. How much you need to put aside for income production at different interest rates is a function of cash flow needs. To find out how much you need to set aside to generate yearly pretax living expenses of X dollars, divide X dollars by the yield you are being offered. Desired Cash Flow divided by the Yield gives you the dollars (assets) you need to invest.

What Comes First?

Determine the demands on your portfolio first. If you have a retirement (or current) income gap, determine the income you would need to take from your portfolio before you commit to any particular investment. Then you can think about the types of bonds that would be best to generate it.

The Tax Effect

In the illustrations in this chapter (and in the next), I have left out the impact of taxes to concentrate on how a demands-based portfolio works. In real life, I would also calculate the effect of taxes before structuring the portfolio. To give you an example of how that might work, let's go back to Marge's mid-risk option, which I discussed on page 30. We figured that Marge would need $320,000 of capital invested at 7.5 percent to produce $24,000 of income. This assumes Marge pays no taxes on the income, which is possible if she invests in tax-free bonds.

Now, let's assume the income is taxable, which is a more likely scenario. Let's see how that capital commitment would change after you accounted for taxes. To keep the math simple, let's use 25 percent as Marge's effective income tax rate. Here is how the math would work. To account for a tax of 25 percent, Marge would need to generate income of $32,000 to be able to spend $24,000. (You arrive at this number by dividing $24,000 by 0.75, which is 1.00 minus the tax rate of 0.25.) The difference ($32,000 minus $24,000 = $8,000), will be your tax bill on the interest income produced by the taxable bond. Now, you solve for $32,000 of income at 7.5 percent. Dividing $32,000 by 7.5 percent (0.075), you get $426,666, which is the amount Marge would need to invest to produce $32,000, leaving her $24,000 to spend after she pays taxes of $8,000. That leaves $573,334 to invest for growth and preservation of capital.

> **TIP**
>
> To find out how much you need to set aside to generate yearly living expenses of X dollars, divide X dollars by the yield you are being offered. Desired Cash Flow divided by the Yield gives you the dollars (assets) you need to invest.

Summary

It is extremely helpful to know how much you need to generate from your portfolio for living expenses. If you know the size of your personal retirement income gap, you can make sound strategic decisions today that will fill the gap in retirement. If you do not know the size of the gap, your ability to fill it in the future will depend entirely on luck—winning a multimillion-dollar lottery, dying young, or raising happy children who can't wait for you to move in with them in your old age. In Chapter 7, I explain how a couple applied the principles we have talked about so far.

Demands-Based Investment Objectives: A Case Study

The example of Tom and Mary illustrates how to set personal investment objectives. Tom plans to retire early and wants to know if he should reduce his stock allocations. This example is a real fact pattern, with identifying information changed.

When Tom started working at a factory in a small New England town after graduating from high school, he made $75 a week. After a layoff, he realized he might not have control over his job situation and might never have the opportunity to stay at a company long enough to qualify, or *vest*, in a pension plan. So he saved and invested regularly on his own and through an IRA, and much later, a 401(k) at work.

Now 55, Tom and his wife, Mary, have $1 million, split about equally between their tax-deferred and taxable accounts. The taxable account has about $50,000 Connecticut municipal bonds, $50,000 taxable bonds, with the remainder in stocks. The 401(k) and IRAs have about $150,000 in government bonds and bond mutual funds and the rest is in individual stocks and stock mutual funds.

Tom and Mary want to retire in five years at the age of 60. They want to be prepared financially as they enter into their last five years of employment. "Stocks have done a good job for us and now 75 percent of our holdings are in stocks and stock mutual funds," they say. "The first thing we want to know is whether we should lower our stock allocations. We want to be safe rather than sorry as we move closer to retirement."

Lowering the stock allocation would protect Tom and Mary from stock market swings, but it would also lessen the potential for continued long-term growth. Left to their own devices, most people come up with an arbitrary allocation. Working with a portfolio manager, an allocation would be figured based on the demands of the portfolio over their lifetime. Let me give you an idea of how that is done.

Demands of the Portfolio

The first question to ask is how Tom and Mary want to use the portfolio after they retire. Tom and Mary considered changes they wanted in their lifestyle. With grandchildren in the area, they were certain they did not want to move or travel. They felt they would be happy with a slow, lazy, low-key life of sailing and fishing on the Long Island Sound with friends and family. They figured they needed about $50,000 a year to pay for their living expenses in today's dollars. This included real estate taxes on the $300,000 home they owned free and clear. But, it did not include income taxes. *Income taxes need to be figured after allocations are made, since allocation decisions may result in taxable, tax deferred, or tax-free investments.*

Sources of Income

Tom has a company pension that will begin at age 60. It will pay him $12,000 a year. Tom and Mary are looking to their 401(k)s, IRAs, and joint brokerage account to make up the difference, and to keep up with inflation.

If Tom were 65 today, after having contributed at the maximum Social Security level, he would have a Social Security benefit of about $16,000 a year. To simplify this discussion, however, because we are concentrating on allocations, we will leave aside the Social Security benefits Tom and Mary will be receiving. Social Security is covered in Chapter 30.

So, Tom and Mary's portfolio would have to produce enough money to cover the gap between what they are taking in (their pension income and later, Social Security) and what they are spending (their living expenses).

While taxes and Social Security need to be worked into the equation as discussed, let's use $38,000 ($50,000 needed less $12,000 pension) for purposes of this illustration. Accordingly, the demands on the portfolio are $38,000 a year of income, increasing by inflation, for their lifetime.

In general, you should follow these portfolio allocation rules:

- Live off the interest and dividend income produced by the portfolio for as long as possible. Avoid selling your investments solely for the purpose of raising cash for living expenses.

- Use taxable investments before tax-deferred dollars. This rule does not always apply in the case of a multimillion-dollar portfolio that you will not outlive. Without appropriate distribution planning (discussed in Chapter 29), dying while holding onto a tax-deferred account can be costly in terms of estate and income tax consequences.

- Make appropriate accommodations for loss of purchasing power over time. Rising costs due to inflation need to be taken into account and offset with a strategy to add to the cash flow produced by the portfolio over a lifetime. You can accomplish this result in different ways, one of which is putting aside money for growth and later restructuring those holdings for income.

- Plan to live long, at least into your 80s.

Based on these rules, how would the money be allocated? Consider the period immediately after retirement from age 60 to 65. First consider how much capital you would need to put to work in a risk-free investment. That is, how much capital you would need to produce a yearly risk-free cash flow of $38,000. You could accomplish that by investing in short-term U.S. Treasury bills, which in the then current interest rate environment would call for about $850,000 of capital. Tom and Mary would have $150,000 left over for growth. But, that wouldn't be enough to solve long-term income needs as those needs rise due to inflation.

Increasing the risk level of the income investments by shifting to corporate bonds would lower the capital commitment needed to produce $38,000 to about $600,000. That would leave $400,000 for growth. Assuming an even higher level of risk in high-yield, low-rated bonds is also possible but not wise in this situation, since the reward is not worth the risk of possible loss of principal due to bond default.

This type of analysis provides a demands-based approach to asset allocation. With it, you can factor in risk and diversification concerns and come up with a final allocation with the overriding objective being to have the portfolio support you throughout your lifetime.

There are three allocation periods to consider regarding retirement security in this scenario:

1. The time between 60 and 65, before full retirement benefits from Social Security income will augment income.

2. Between 65 and 70½ when IRA and 401(k) assets can continue growing tax deferred.

3. Finally, after age 70½ when mandatory distributions add another wrinkle: readjusting allocations to accommodate the burden of mandatory distributions from the IRA and 401(k) accounts (mandatory distributions are covered in Chapter 28).

NOTE

You may work for a company that offers both pretax and after-tax 401(k) accounts. If you contribute on a pretax basis, the money you contribute is not taxed to you as income and does not show up on your W-2.

The portfolio allocation rules are meant to pay your bills while protecting your principal for as long as possible. Of course, you may need to use principal at some point, but it is better not to start out that way. The rules are also meant to keep tax deferral benefits intact as long as possible, to enable growth unfettered by taxes.

For the next five years until he is 60, Tom is planning to continue funding his 401(k) to the maximum permitted by his company's plan and investing in stocks and stock mutual funds. He is putting away $10,000 per year in a pretax 401(k) account, which is being matched with $6,000 by his company; and he is maximizing his supplemental retirement plan, which brings his annual 401(k) and supplemental contribution to $22,500. That will add an additional $100,000 of new money to his overall portfolio by the time he retires at 60.

Tom should rightfully be concerned about the fluctuations of the stock market. His current overall allocation of 75 percent stocks gives him substantial exposure in the event of a sharp correction or a long protracted bear market before retirement.

If he wants to be very cautious, he can lower his equity exposure in his taxable brokerage account to zero and start investing for income in short-term U.S. government obligations, while reinvesting the income until retirement. Ideally, Tom and Mary's tax-deferred monies would remain invested until mandatory distributions begin after age 70½. That allows for a much longer recovery period (from age 55 to age 70½) should markets be unfavorable.

Following allocation rules will help you get a better fix on your decisions before you make them. When moving into retirement, it pays to take some time and do some planning and figuring. Any projecting into the future has limited usefulness, however, since markets, interest rates, and inflation and personal circumstances change. So, refiguring really has to be done regularly, perhaps even yearly. At the same time, it is good to assess taxes on income generated by the portfolio, as well as capital gains tax issues involved when rebalancing outside a tax-deferred account. And, don't forget about estate tax planning as well. We'll discuss income and capital gains taxes in Chapter 25 and estate taxes in Chapter 31.

> **TIP**
>
> Following allocation rules will help you get a better fix on your decisions before you make them.

Tom and Mary's story shows how to make the most of what you have as well. They contribute to their IRAs each year. Tom is contributing to his 401(k) at a level that triggers the maximum match. And, he set up an outside investment account with a brokerage firm to invest on a taxable basis. The mortgage is paid off, as well as college tuition for two children and the boat in the dock. I asked them their secret.

"Well, we knew we had to take care of our pensions because of all my moves, said Tom. So, we started early. We were consistent. And, really, it was just a matter of doing a little at a time and enjoying the opportunities that came our way."

Summary

You, too, can review your situation and your holdings to plan your own portfolio. This account of Tom and Mary is an example of how to approach the project. Take one step at a time, and a picture of what you need to do will unfold as you consider your needs and how to provide for them.

CHAPTER 8

Portfolio Strategy

There is a difference between investing and playing the market. Playing ignores risk and tends to be reactionary—you buy a stock you hear about on a sales call you get at dinnertime, or buy a stock based on a tip from a friend, or buy a moving stock online. Investing involves having a plan that factors in risks and potential rewards. Players do win big from time to time. But, investors have more money in the end, when it counts.

If you have *serious money*, which I define as any sum of money large enough to be important to you, you will want to be an investor. Your ability to invest in accordance with a thought-out plan becomes essential after 50. In fact, setting a personal portfolio strategy for yourself is one of the most important skills you need to develop at this time of life.

Staying the Course

A personal investment strategy focuses your activity on a goal and provides you with a means of getting there. Having a workable strategy helps at all times, but probably most of all when events are occurring that may distract you, such as a current fad or a spectacular move in a market. A good strategy that takes into account different types of markets, will keep you from wandering from the goal, or worse, being drawn away by a smooth-talking salesperson or the breathless fervor of a speculative market.

CAUTION

Playing the market ignores risk and is reactive in nature, while investing involves having a plan that factors in risks and potential rewards.

Winning

Strategically, you want to win the war. That means that you understand you will probably lose some battles along the way. While the stock market is not your opponent, there are professional traders in the market who can and will outmaneuver individual investors most, if not all, of the time.

Institutional traders have access to large sums of money as well as infinitely greater and more sophisticated resources, and they are paid to spend every working minute finding inefficiencies in the market and taking advantage of them. And, more important than anything else, they are not risking their own money. Encouraged by big bonuses for successful trading records, the professional trader's assessment of risk is quite different from the individual investor's. If you try to play the game at an institutional trader's level, you will undoubtedly lose.

Goal

To work, an effective strategy must produce desired results, be simple in concept, and easy to execute. To produce desired results, you should start with the end in mind. That is the goal. The goal with the highest priority for most people is to produce enough money to live on throughout retirement. You may also have a secondary goal, such as, leaving an inheritance for your children.

NOTE

Strategically, you want to win the war. That means you will probably lose some battles along the way.

Knowing the goal does not tell you how to reach it. One of the tools I use to teach personal investment strategy is time travel. Really. Instead of using a crystal ball to predict what will happen, you travel ahead in time to let's say, age 85. See yourself living a safe, secure, and happy life, having successfully met your investment goals. Now, look in a rearview mirror to see how you got there.

Next, imagine not having made the right savings and investment choices. Where are you living? What resources do you have? Do you feel secure? With this knowledge, is there anything that you would do differently today?

Most people who go through this exercise find that they could be making better decisions today. No matter what age, people wish they had started investing earlier. They wish they had spent time learning how to invest. Those with 401(k) plans wish they had maximized their company matches.

> **TIP**
>
> To work, an effective strategy must produce desired results, be simple in concept, and easy to execute.

The Life-Cycle Strategy

Let me introduce a strategy I call the Three-Phase Life Cycle which sets your *primary* investment objectives for the rest of your life. Each phase has its own set of investment rules. Sticking to them will help you avoid sleepless nights when stock prices drop from time to time.

Starting with the end in mind, in Phase 3 when you are retired, you are investing for income. In Phase 2, just before retirement, you are starting to acquire income-producing investments. In Phase 1, when you are young, you are investing for growth to build your portfolio.

Starting from the beginning, first you invest for growth. Later, as you approach retirement, you start to rebalance into income-producing investments. Finally, you invest for income. In the spirit of time travel, let's skip to income production.

Phase 3: Investing for Income

At some point in the future, you will want your investment portfolio to pay you a stream of "pension" checks throughout your retirement, which may last for 30 years or longer. For most people, this is the real reason for investing—to use the income it produces to support retirement.

When you do retire, you will be using this stream of income to live on or to supplement your pension. Your job in Phase 3 is to create income from your portfolio, which is done primarily through income-producing investments such as bonds. *You want to have your income-producing investments cover your retirement needs as much as possible, because you want to avoid selling off principal, especially in a correction or a bear market.*

The percentage of your Phase 3 portfolio that you need to invest in income-producing investments during your retirement will depend on your particular situation: things we've talked about in previous chapters—how much you need for living expenses; the amount of your pension, Social Security benefits, and other resources; and the importance of your portfolio in making up any shortfall between income and expenses. Your portfolio may actually need to have 80 percent or more in bonds if you must rely heavily on it for income or 20 percent or less in bonds if you can rely on other sources for income.

If you are currently in retirement and are taking money out of interest or dividends created by your portfolio, a correction or bear market will have little effect on you. You will be in trouble, however, if you did not rebalance your portfolio before reaching retirement.

Phase 2: Rebalancing

Rebalancing is sandwiched between accumulation and withdrawal. During this transitional time of roughly five years before retirement, you are slowly adding income-producing holdings and also converting some of your growth holdings to income-producing holdings. Of the three phases of the investment life cycle, the rebalancing phase is the hardest, since it takes planning and discipline.

> **NOTE**
>
> **Of the three phases of the investment life cycle, the rebalancing phase is the hardest to execute, since it takes planning and discipline.**

Over the rebalancing phase, your objective is to acquire income-producing investments that you will use to pay yourself income during retirement, while maintaining some of your stock positions to continue to grow your portfolio.

If you are exchanging your stock for bonds during a bear market or correction, you will want to wait until the market stabilizes, so that you don't sell those holdings at a loss. This is one of the reasons for having a longer, five-year rebalancing horizon.

Phase 1: Investing for Growth

Think of Phase 1 as the booster rocket that places a satellite in orbit. In Phase 1, your job is to grow your portfolio to a size that is large enough for you to live on in retirement. In this phase, you would invest primarily in growth investments such as stocks, and ride out the ups and downs of the market.

In Phase 1, it is not your job to time the market or to try to beat the market. Your job is simply to accumulate assets for retirement. You may have 10 or 20 years, or more, *until* retirement and you may have another 30 years of retirement. You will have to contend with numerous up-and-down periods of the market. If you follow my investment life-cycle method, however, you will not have to change course during a correction or a bear market.

Summary

Following the life cycle can help you put your investment objectives in perspective. Important, the life cycle keeps you from selling at a loss in a down market because the market will be irrelevant until you begin to withdraw funds during retirement. At that time, you should be safely withdrawing income, not principal, from income-producing instruments.

> **NOTE**
>
> In Phase 1, your job is to grow your portfolio to a size that is large enough for you to live on in retirement.

CHAPTER 9

Monitoring and Reviewing Results

Even with the best-laid strategies, perfect asset allocations, and sound investments, you can still fail to meet your goals. How can that be? The answer lies in understanding that making money in the financial markets depends on a series of correct decisions. Successful investing is a process, not a single set of acts. Since no one can bat 1,000, the key to success is recognizing when you are off course and making corrections as quickly as possible.

The only way to do that is to regularly review objectives—growth, income, and preservation of capital—and measure performance against those objectives. If your current income objective is to produce cash flow of $10,000 a year, add up the interest or dividend distributions you received for the year from the income portion of your portfolio. Did they total $10,000?

Regular reviews allow you to make appropriate adjustments to your portfolio as needed. Set up a realistic schedule, but conduct a review at the very least once each year; once each quarter is a better goal. Just as a pilot regularly checks his instruments to maintain his desired direction, altitude, and speed, so must a successful investor be vigilant in monitoring the information that tells him how he is doing.

By describing my general approach to the monitoring and review of a portfolio, I can help you develop a simple system of your own if you are not working with a personal money manager. My goal in monitoring the portfolio is to make sure the investments are performing as expected. My goal in reviewing a portfolio with the client is to confirm that it is indeed meeting the client's objectives.

Objectives are always the starting point since they govern how the portfolio is structured and managed. The objectives are normally set out in writing and are included in a report we provide the client, along with an investment policy that states how we intend to meet the objectives. If you were withdrawing cash from the portfolio, we would normally include a written cash withdrawal policy as well. The performance of the portfolio would then be measured against these policy statements. Over time, the policy statements would need to be adapted to reflect changes in circumstance, experience, or goals.

Monitoring

Monitoring the portfolio entails three levels of scrutiny, all of which the client may or may not see, depending on the client's level of interest in the process:

1. The top level requires looking at the overall portfolio, adding together all the accounts that are being managed.

2. At the second level, you must monitor each component of the portfolio by investment objective.

3. The third level involves looking at each individual position held in each account.

We look at data from the inception of each account as well as the most recent reporting period, which can be the last quarter or the last month, depending on the portfolio. On the first two levels, we are looking at performance against objectives. On the third level, we are looking for deviations from expectations—we want to see if the holding is performing as expected or needs to be replaced. In doing so, we compare the holding to *benchmarks* and to similar holdings.

For growth investments, we consider total returns including capital appreciation and reinvested distributions. For investments used to generate income withdrawn from the account by the client, we measure the amount of income produced and the risk level assumed to produce that level of income. While we are measuring returns, we are also measuring volatility of the overall portfolio, the accounts, and the individual holdings. To put risk in real terms, we use a proprietary risk measure we call *downside exposure*, which we developed to assess the overall risk of the portfolio in dollars and cents. For example, based on our assessment of the risk level of the portfolio, we estimate how much the client can lose due to risk exposure. The current value of the portfolio might be $1 million. The downside exposure might be $150,000, which tells the client that he might expect the portfolio to drop to $850,000 in a normal market.

> **NOTE**
>
> A benchmark is a meaningful comparative measure of performance. For large capitalization stocks, a common benchmark is the S&P 500 Index.

Review

If you were a client, we would meet in person or by phone each review period to discuss the following four agenda items. We like to follow the same agenda every meeting, while adding items that may come up in individual cases:

1. Whether there have been any changes in the client's circumstances since our last meeting. Perhaps a client has decided to take an early retirement and will be needing to generate an income stream for himself sooner than he thought. Or, a client may need cash to build a summer home. Or, he may need to increase monthly cash flow from the portfolio. Since changes in needs might call for a change in the investment objectives, we need to know this up front.

2. A review of the portfolio in light of the investment policy, risk level, and purpose of the portfolio. We check to see if the overall results are what we expect. Is enough income being produced?

Is enough allocated for growth? Do allocations need to be adjusted? Is enough or too much risk being assumed?

3. An assessment of the continued suitability of the portfolio for meeting the client's goals. This part of the discussion helps us confirm one more time whether the portfolio is on track for meeting the client's objectives. That is the purpose of a personal review.

4. Other issues. This is a catchall to pick up any other matters the client wishes us to consider. Many times we assist the client in obtaining appropriate legal, estate planning, or tax advice. For example, if a mandatory distribution needs to be made from an IRA account, we coordinate with the client's tax attorney or accountant in reviewing the various decisions available to the client and their possible consequences.

> **NOTE**
>
> Time weighted return (TWR) is a portfolio accounting method that measures investment performance (income + price changes) as a percentage of capital "at work," without taking into account additions and withdrawals of capital. This return is useful when comparing an investment to a benchmark. Dollar-weighted return is a portfolio accounting method that measures investment performance (income + price changes) as a percentage of capital "at work," taking into account your additions and withdrawals of capital. The dollar-weighted return should not be used to compare an investment to a benchmark.

Standards

Professional money managers are held to a standard published by the Association of Investment Management and Research (AIMR). Portfolio management and reporting software that managers use to report performance to their clients follows AIMR standards.

To be in compliance, the manager's performance numbers must present total returns and time-weighted rates of return. *Time-weighted returns* remove the impact of money flows into and out of the portfolio and, because of that, are useful in comparing the performance of one manager to another. *Dollar-weighted returns* take into account the size and timing of cash flows into and out of the account and thus reflect your actual performance. The problem with dollar-weighted returns is that comparisons to benchmarks will not be accurate.

Your Own System

You need to develop your own monitoring system if you invest on your own or through a stockbroker, financial planner, insurance salesperson, or banker, since many of these advisers do partial tracking or no tracking at all. In a recent lawsuit against a stockbroker for unsuitable trading, the broker reported only realized gains for stocks the client sold at a profit. The broker did not report unrealized losses for stocks the client still held in her brokerage account. The client thought she was making money. She was unaware that if she had included the stocks she still owned, she was hundreds of thousands of dollars behind.

The first step in developing your own monitoring system is getting your bearings. Establish your own objectives, write them down, and ignore what your friends are doing with their investments. A trap that often takes people off course is making investments a topic of social conversation. In the technology market of 1999 and early 2000, many conservative investors were drawn into highly speculative trading because of what they heard on 24-hour news programs and from boastful friends. Keep in mind that some people exaggerate their wins. Others don't mention their losses. Most importantly, remember your own goals and don't bother with anyone else's.

NOTE

An unrealized gain/loss is a paper gain/loss. It becomes a realized gain or loss when the security is actually sold.

Second, performance reviews present an opportunity to reconsider why you bought an investment in light of the overall picture. Make sure you understand the purpose the investment is serving in your portfolio. What role did you expect the holding to play in your overall portfolio? Is it doing what you expected?

The way to do this is to keep track of investment decisions, why you made them when you did, and what you expected any particular investment to do for you. Keep a ledger of the details of each purchase (price, date, cost, commission), the purpose of the holding in your portfolio, and what you expect it to do for you. Each quarter, calculate the return and compare it against at least one appropriate benchmark.

For large company stocks, the best measure is the S&P 500 Index, which is published by Standard & Poor's and reported in the newspapers and online. Comparing your stocks and stock funds to the S&P

500 will give you a sense of how you did compared to the stock market as a whole.

However, the S&P 500 Index is not a meaningful measure for a portfolio that is meant to produce income. If all your holdings are allocated to income production, which you use for living expenses, you need another meaningful measure. I might measure your results in three ways. First, did the portfolio satisfy your need for safety? Second, did the income produced satisfy your need for income? Third, was the safety-to-income relationship representative of other similar investments you could have made?

Focus on losing positions in particular and compare them to similar investments. An investment with disappointing results needs to be understood or dealt with. Focusing on losing positions will help you determine when to sell, hold, or buy more, which is probably one of the hardest skills to learn. It's much better to apply a dispassionate set of criteria to weed out your losers than to cross your fingers and hope your losing positions will recover. Chapter 14 focuses on how to set up your own criteria.

TIP

Establish your own objectives, write them down, and ignore what your friends are doing with their investments.

Finally, assess risk. One way to get yourself into trouble is failing to see your investment for what it is. Risk needs to be understood and balanced against potential reward. Performance may give you some clues that you may have misjudged the risk of a holding compared with what you expect it can do for you. Take an extreme example. You invested all your retirement money in the stock of the company you work for because you thought it was a safe investment. If it starts to drop in price while other companies in the industry are holding steady or rising, pay attention to performance. It is telling you that the investment presents a greater risk than you might have thought.

Your System

Your system has to be easy to use. At a minimum, you might list the following on a piece of paper each quarter:

- When, how much, and why did you invest in each investment?
- What level of risk did you assume? You can find risk assessments such as standard deviation in different market research publications, such as Value Line, Morningstar, and Standard & Poor's.

- What is it worth today?
- What is the cumulative return on the investment since you bought it? Annualized?
- How does that compare with other similar investments?
- What is your return after commissions, and other costs?
- What is your return after taxes?
- How does this compare with the S&P 500 Index, or another appropriate benchmark?

If you buy more of a single investment over a period of time, treat each new purchase as a brand-new investment.

> **TIP**
>
> It's much better to apply a dispassionate set of criteria to weed out your losers than to cross your fingers and hope your losing positions will recover.

Summary

When monitoring your portfolio, you need to know where you are starting, where you are headed, and whether you are on course. Just as the wind can take an airplane off course, so do the workings of the Federal Reserve, the markets, earnings reports, wars, and a multitude of other factors that you may not even consider. Like a pilot, you need to check and correct, check and correct, check and correct, over and over as time goes on. If you do this, your investing will be a success.

CHAPTER 10

Risk

Your Risk Profile

The financial services industry uses a tool called the *risk profile*, which you see most often in 401(k) educational literature. Ostensibly, if you know your risk profile, you will know how much risk you want to assume. As with many tools that try to oversimplify a multivariate problem, I find the risk profile ineffective, partly because honesty would call for a low risk profile. No one *wants* to lose money.

Understanding and working with risk is another matter. There are times in your life when you really need to fully understand how much damage a wrong decision can cause. One of those times is when you are investing irreplaceable assets after the age of 50. I recently came across a situation that illustrates this point.

An economist invested a large inheritance in a "risk-free" stock market investment that he understood was guaranteed not to lose money. When asked, he was not sure exactly what he had bought. He did not know how the guarantee worked. He did not know how much the adviser got paid to sell him the product, nor that there was a substantial penalty attached if he wanted to take money out before a certain time.

While he had thought about these questions at the time of the purchase, the economist told me that he was too embarrassed to ask them. I share this story to those of you who feel awkward asking questions for fear of showing ignorance. When you are investing, you are probably facing a highly trained salesperson who might want to make you feel he knows more than you do. Don't let that stop you from getting the answers. I also want to emphasize that education and even a work history in finance does not make you an expert at everything. You are expected to ask about risk, costs, and expectations, especially if the selling point is something you would not expect: a "no-risk" investment. I often ask questions that would make someone else embarrassed, and the less sophisticated the questions, the more information I usually get. I also ask to see these types of promises in writing. Chapters 18 and 19 will help you develop some good interviewing skills.

Risk-Free Investing?

When you make an investment, you part with your money with the expectation that some day in the future, you will get more back, but this may or may not be the case. The future outcome of your investment is uncertain and risk is unavoidable. Risk is an integral element of any investment.

If risk were taken out of the investment, you would have what is called a *perfect hedge*. In a perfect hedge, you invest in two or more forms of investment that offset each other's risk assumptions in perfect parity. Once the hedge is put into place, you know exactly what you will get back in the future.

Hedges are used everyday by farmers who buy futures contracts to lock in prices for the crops they will bring to market later in the season. While perfection is hard to achieve in reality, it is something strived for. Unless you have other reasons, such as protecting the current value of a large company stock grant, you would not want to take the risk out of the investment. By doing so, you would also take out the potential for gain. Without risk, there is no investment.

Assuming Risk

Given that you need to assume risk when you invest, you need to understand what to expect. In some cases, an investment puts all your money at risk, which means that in the worst case, you can lose everything you invest. With some investments, you can actually lose more than you invest. For example, if you buy a stock on margin, write options, sell a stock short, or buy or sell futures contracts, you can owe the brokerage firm money if the value of your investment sinks below the value of your collateral. Before you assume the risk of any investment, find out how much you stand to lose after costs and penalties.

Professional money managers applying modern portfolio theory look for ways to measure risk, such as standard deviation. Standard deviation allows us to see the probability and depth of a bad outcome. In my practice, I use the standard deviation of a particular holding when computing what I call *downside exposure*, and then translate that figure into a total dollar loss potential of the portfolio, which gives me a rough idea of how much a client's portfolio could fall due to normal expectations at any given point in time. This is not an absolute loss point, but a probability. The

NOTE

One standard deviation gives you a read on what happens two out of three times. Two standard deviations reflect 95 percent of the occurrences in a series.

number represents what we expect to happen two out of three times, and is based on one standard deviation. We find downside exposure useful in helping a client understand how much risk he is assuming at any point in time, with the caveat that actual losses can be far greater (3 standard deviations).

To illustrate, if a client understands that his portfolio, as structured, is expected to fall from $1 million to $850,000 from time to time, it helps him understand how much risk he is taking at any point in time. If this is too much for the client to bear, the portfolio can be adjusted using lower risk investments, thus lowering the downside exposure of the portfolio. For example, we can restructure the $1 million portfolio for a downside expectation of $900,000 by adding 3-month U.S. Treasury bills. For someone who wants minimal downside exposure, we can structure a portfolio entirely of short-term 3-month U.S. Treasuries, which will preserve capital, but provide no growth. Assuming no Treasury bills had to be sold before maturity, that portfolio would be risk-free from a volatility point of view. In Nobel Prize winner Harry Markowitz's terms, if safety is of extreme importance, we are sacrificing return to decrease uncertainty. You give up growth; you get preservation of capital. The remaining risk would be limited to inflation and taxes.

Speculation

The short-term online trader often tries to make the most money in the shortest amount of time—without considering uncertainty of return. This is a valid objective for a speculative risk-oriented trader. It moves him to look for opportunities for big stock price movements in high volume. If skilled, the trader will sell quickly out of losing positions and let the winners ride. There may be a lot of trading for quick profits. And, there is the significant risk of a crash-and-burn outcome, many times because the trader ignores downside exposure.

NOTE

Harry Markowitz is widely regarded as the father of modern portfolio theory. In 1990, he was awarded the Nobel Prize for economics.

Consider this Internet software company. The stock opened the year 2000 at $85 a share, and dropped 40 percent by February 28. From there, it shot up 64 percent to its high of the year. By May 15, the stock was at $13, a drop of 84 percent from the former high it set on March 10. In comparison, an investment of $100 in an S&P 500 Index fund would have seen a drop to $91 by the end of February, a jump to $105 by March 23, back down to $93 in April, ending at $96 by May 15. Pricey stocks with negligible earnings and low or no profits are a buying opportunity only for the most speculative of traders.

Insight from Academia

A great body of academic work focuses on risk in the financial markets. Markowitz posited the investor's dilemma (wanting a high return and no risk of loss) in his work, *Portfolio Selection: Efficient Diversification of Investments* (copyright 1959; re-released by Blackwell Publishers, 1991). Originally published as his doctoral thesis, the work set out to explain portfolio risk and forms the basis of modern portfolio theory.

According to Markowitz:

Uncertainty is a salient feature of security investment. Economic forces are not understood well enough for predictions to be beyond doubt or error. Even if the consequences of economic conditions were understood perfectly, non-economic influences can change the course of general prosperity, the level of the market, or the success of a particular security. The health of the President, changes in international tensions, increases or decreases in military spending, an extremely dry summer,

the successes of an invention, the miscalculation of a business management—all can affect the capital gains or dividends of one of many securities. We are expecting too much if we require the securities analyst
to predict with certainty whether a typical security will increase or
decrease in value. . . . Only the clairvoyant could hope to predict with
certainty.

Conflict

As Markowitz says, two objectives are common to all investors. At
the same time that they want return to be high, they want return to be
"dependable, stable and not subject to uncertainty." And, therein lies
the conflict of the investor: how to achieve high return and low risk
at the same time. "The portfolio with the highest likely return is not
necessarily the one with the least uncertainty of return," according to
Markowitz. Markowitz did not end the inquiry there. He offered a solution. Investing in an efficient manner lessened risk and increased
the likelihood of return. This theory forms the basis for later academic studies that further developed the efficient market theory and
helped formulate risk measures such as beta, alpha, and standard deviation and concepts such as diversification and correlation.

Academics who have studied the financial markets have developed pricing models that attribute the risk of an investment in part
to market risk or *systemic* risk and in part to company-specific risk
or *unsystemic* risk. These concepts are developed in the capital
asset pricing model developed by Nobel Prize winner, William F.
Sharpe, professor of finance at Stanford University. Much of the investment industry relies on this model in assessing the risk-reward
characteristics of an asset class or a particular investment. According to Frank Fabozzi, formerly professor of finance at MIT's Sloan
School of Management, and author of *Investment Management*
(see the Appendix), the assumption on which this theory rests is
that markets are efficient.

Market prices reflect the presence, size, and scope of professional
traders and arbitrageurs in the marketplace. Given their ability to act
more quickly on previous prices and publicly available information
than the public, pricing inefficiencies coming to their attention are
short-lived. An individual has no opportunity to take advantage of inefficiencies, and thus must, can, and should work with the market, rather
than try to outsmart it, which will prove to be a fruitless exercise.

New investors may seek to make a profit on an investment by looking for a good deal that does not exist, such as a 15 percent yield on a bond when all others of like risk pay only 5 percent. An uninitiated investor can find a 15 percent coupon and think it is the yield he would earn on the investment, not understanding that in a 5 percent market, you would be paying a premium for the bond. Bond pricing is discussed in Chapter 16. Market efficiency ultimately means that it is "impossible to make abnormal profit (other than by chance)."

NOTE

If you are paying a premium for a bond, that means you are paying more than the face value. If you are paying $2,000 for a $1,000 bond, you are paying a premium.

Summary

Risk is a difficult issue to tackle. It is inevitable, and in fact, it is desirable. Without risk, you cannot expect to make a profit. In your own personal situation, your job is to understand the risk you are assuming in each investment you make, as well as the risk of your overall portfolio. We talk about risk some more in the chapters dealing with stocks, bonds, and money market instruments. Risk also includes the loss of purchasing power due to inflation, taxes, and other factors, such as costs, that influence your real return. In the next chapter, let's discuss how to manage your portfolio.

CHAPTER 11

The Job of Managing Your Portfolio

Portfolio management is different from stock picking, which you can either do on your own through a discount broker, with a full-service stockbroker at a major Wall Street firm, with your banker, financial planner, or even with your accountant in the states that permit accountants to engage in commissioned sales. You have several options as to how to approach the management of your portfolio from this day forward.

You may be used to working with professionals and wish to retain a personal portfolio manager. Or, you may wish to serve as your own portfolio manager while working with brokers to execute your trades. What skills, background, and characteristics would you look for in a professional or in yourself, if you were to act as your own manager?

The essential job that your personal portfolio manager should do for you is fivefold:

1. To help you articulate a portfolio strategy based on your particular circumstances and needs for the present and with a view to the future.

2. To organize the portfolio to meet your particular objectives.

3. To supervise the investments and review them regularly and replace them as necessary.

4. To monitor your portfolio to make sure those objectives are being met.

5. To review the portfolio with you periodically and adapt it to your objectives as they change over time.

The value of a good personal portfolio manager is the organization and discipline he brings to the enterprise, and this is in essence the professional service you pay for. As in every professional relationship, you expect a certain level of knowledge and skill will be brought to bear on your behalf. You can also expect a relationship in which there are few, if any, conflicting agendas.

TIP

The value of a good personal portfolio manager is the organization and discipline he brings to the enterprise, and this is in essence the professional service you pay for.

Assuming you find the required level of skill, knowledge, and honesty, the ability to understand each other and agree on philosophical grounds becomes extremely important. Personalities need to complement each other. There has to be mutual respect and an understanding of common goals. Mutual responsibilities and expectations have to be understood and agreed on. These are the "soft" characteristics of a working relationship that cannot be defined up front. They can only be discovered after getting to know the person you will be working with.

Let me dispel the idea that you should look for someone you can trust. I am a firm believer that you should trust no one until the trust is earned through a period of observation and working together. Training materials used in the securities industry include examples that help salespersons learn to use words that will elicit a trust response from a prospect. A training manual for a well-known limited partnership sold through a major Wall Street brokerage firm in the late 1980s taught brokers to assess their prospects and categorize them as "feeling types" versus "skeptics." For the feeling prospects, salespersons were taught to use words such as "I understand," "I feel you're right," "trust me," "we're in this together." With the skeptics, salespersons were taught to say, "we'll have to check on that," and so on.

Sources

When I am looking for expertise, I search through professional publications and organizations, particularly committees focused on the areas of expertise that I want to find. For example, if I go to a bar association and ask for the chair of the trusts and estates committee, I can be assured of finding a lawyer who is versed in trusts and estates. I cannot use the same process to find a personal portfolio manager, because professional money managers do not tend to participate in organizations comparable to bar associations. Financial planning organizations do exist as do accountant organizations that have financial planning committees, but I am distinguishing portfolio managers from financial planners and accountants.

Publications may be a possible resource, solely because you can get a feel for the philosophy of the writer. But here again, I do not think this will be an adequate resource for most people. Advertising in general is probably not a way to find a good manager.

When I think of how people find our firm, I can't say that we make it easy for them. We have a slow growth philosophy that does not allow us to advertise, hire salespeople, or pay referral fees. A client's accountant or attorney will refer someone to us as will a friend or acquaintance of an existing client. And, perhaps that is the best way to find someone to work with if you are looking. That is, you may ask a trusted friend, your accountant, or your attorney for a referral. Watch out for self-referral though.

> **CAUTION**
>
> I am a firm believer that you should trust no one until the trust is earned through a period of observation and working together.

I recommend doing some preparatory work before deciding to search for an adviser. Following these six steps will save you some time and effort:

1. Assess your strengths and weaknesses. If you love the transactional nature of trading, can you slow down enough to allocate assets for the long term? If you rarely open your statements, do you have the discipline to follow your investments? If you do not measure your performance now, will you do so in the future?

2. Assess the importance of your decision to find the right investment adviser. If the assets you wish to invest are irreplaceable, you are more vulnerable to loss. In that event, you need to be more careful in your selection process.

You can turn to the yellow pages to find a landscaper or plumber, but not a financial adviser. Or, you may decide to hire yourself.

3. Understand the skills you need. When you are trading, you need good advice and good execution, which are available through a traditional stockbroker or online. When you are investing irreplaceable assets for retirement, you need an adviser skilled in structuring and managing a portfolio tailored to your specific needs.

In some cases involving pension plans, 401(k) accounts, stock bonus and option plans, and other benefits, you may need a financial team. Your team should include your investment adviser, your tax adviser, your legal adviser, and your employer's benefits specialist.

4. Buyer beware. Understand that you may be pitched by a highly trained salesperson. Some highly skilled salespeople engender feelings of friendship early on in the relationship. Withhold trust until it is earned. And, even then, keep in mind that it is irresponsible to turn yourself over to your adviser.

TIP

The best adviser-client relationship is an arm's-length business relationship based on mutual respect.

The best adviser-client relationship is an arm's-length business relationship based on mutual respect. The adviser does not dominate the relationship, take the upper hand, or make you feel inadequate.

5. If you decide to retain someone, do some research. In Chapter 18, I discuss how advisers are regulated and paid, which helps you distinguish what they will do for you. And in Chapter 20, I provide a list of questions to ask when interviewing a stockbroker.

Get a list of prospects together based on the criteria you are looking for. You might research prospective advisers through friends or colleagues. You might turn to financial literature. If you ask your lawyer or accountant for advice, be sure to find out if there are any referral fees or other incentives or relationships that may influence the referral.

Some accounting firms and law firms are setting up related advisory arms that provide investment advice. This arrangement may increase the likelihood for a potential conflict of interest. I like to see accounting services provided by accountants, legal advice given by lawyers, and investment advice given by investment advisers.

6. Don't rush. If you feel pressure to make a quick decision, you may make a bad move. Take your time to explore possibilities. Choosing the right financial adviser for important assets is like

getting married. It is a long-term relationship. You want to be sure you are compatible before you tie the knot.

Summary

After 50 and especially after retirement, seeing your investments as a portfolio instead of individual holdings will help you make better decisions for your future. Consider the skills and tasks necessary for managing your portfolio, many of which are organizational in nature. If you are strong on assessment, organization, and follow-up, you may be the best person to hire as your own portfolio manager. If you do that, you can work with a reputable stockbroker who can help you pick appropriate investments to fit your objectives. (Working with a broker is covered in Chapter 20.) Or, you may want to research stocks, bonds, and mutual funds on your own using some of the tools discussed in the following chapters.

CAUTION

Choosing the right financial adviser for important assets is like getting married. It is a long-term relationship. You want to be sure you are compatible before you tie the knot.

CHAPTER 12

Investing for Capital Appreciation

If your objective is capital appreciation, you will be looking to the stock market to meet that objective. There are hundreds of sources of information about stocks and stock selection, including hundreds of books; scholarly works; guides; newsletters; research reports; screening software; Internet sites; and television, cable, and radio news programs all with advice for the individual investor. Add to that the people who are willing to give advice, and what you have is a mad mix of gurus hankering for your attention.

In fact, so much information is available that the best advice is to decide on a few sound sources and to ignore the rest. Ultimately, you will have to determine what resources are best for you considering your interests, time, and background. To give you a start in the right direction, I list some reliable resources in the Appendix.

This chapter provides a general overview of three factors that might affect your approach to investing for capital appreciation: (1) your style, (2) the effort you are willing to devote, and (3) whether you should try to beat the market. These preliminary issues really come down to a question of how much time you want to spend at stock selection. In the next chapter, I show you how a research publication written for individual investors can help you gather information about stocks. In Chapter 14, I discuss investment policy and when to sell. Mutual funds are covered in Chapter 15.

Your Goal

To meet your growth objectives, you want to select stocks or stock mutual funds that give you the potential for growth over a defined period of time at acceptable levels of risk. In buying stocks for your portfolio, your goal is to make money at some future date when you sell the stock for a profit. You can also buy stocks that pay dividends for income purposes. There are thousands of domestic and foreign stocks from which to choose as well as thousands of mutual funds that invest in stocks.

Personal Style and Time Horizon

Before you can set a course for buying stocks, it is a good idea to consider your basis for picking stock investments. Your personal views will determine how you want to approach investing. There are two basic styles to choose from: *value* and *growth*. Warren Buffett, whom we first met in Chapter 2, is viewed as a value investor. If you are a value investor, you may like the idea of buying the undervalued stock of a well-managed company that you can hold for the long term for its potential rise in price. If you are a growth investor, you may be willing to pay more for stock since you are looking for stocks that are in rapid growth stages and promise a quicker profit.

NOTE

Your time horizon needs to be considered before making a growth investment. Unless you are a skilled stock trader, it is better to take the safer route and lessen the risk level of your portfolio if you need your principal a short time after you invest it.

Value investors tend to buy a stock when it is priced right (i.e., when it is viewed to be cheap) and to hold the stock, sometimes indefinitely. One measure of the relative price of a stock is determined by comparing price-to-book value or P/B; another is price-to-earnings or P/E. To calculate these ratios, you divide the market price of the stock into the earnings or book value, as appropriate. Earnings are reported by the company in its financial statements and represent the company's profit. Book value is a reflection of the breakup value of the company itself. Book value per share is the net worth of the company, less preferred stock at liquidating value, divided by the common shares outstanding.

If the stock has a low P/B and low P/E, it may attract the attention of value investors. Of course, the lower relative price of a value stock is not a guarantee that it will not decline further from the purchase price. Part of the assumption of the value investor is that you have to wait to reap your rewards. Value investing tends to be a long-term strategy.

Growth investors would rather look for current success and tend to buy stocks that are exhibiting growth trends measured by earnings growth, sales growth, and the like, irrespective of current price. A stock that is overvalued (high P/B and high P/E), may still be attractive to growth investors if it has potential for growth. This can be estimated in several ways, some of which are discussed in Chapter 13.

> **NOTE**
>
> Book value is a reflection of the breakup value of the company itself. Book value per share is the net worth of the company, less preferred stock at liquidating value, divided by the common shares outstanding.

To get a feel for how pricey the market is as a whole, you can look at the S&P 500 Index, which is a measure of the broad market. As of the end of 2000, according to Morningstar, the P/E for the S&P 500 Index was 31.6 while the P/B was 7.7. The average P/E for the previous five years was 29.8, with a five-year low of 18.8 and a five-year high of 34.3. The average P/B for the previous five years was 6.4, with a five-year low of 4.1 and a five-year high of 6.5. You can compare your own stocks to these broad market measures for a quick read on where your stock stands in terms of relative value.

Relative value alone will not determine whether you should buy. It will just tell you that a stock is cheap or costly. Knowing the distinction will help you set a time horizon for the stock. If you can see yourself as someone who wants to buy for long-term potential, you would want to select value stocks. If you want to buy for short-term profit taking, you might look to growth stocks. The discussion of selection tools in Chapter 13 includes some examples of growth and value stocks and how to find them.

Effort and Attention

David L. Dodd, coauthor of the classic investment text, *Security Analysis, Principles and Technique* (McGraw-Hill Book, 1934) and author of *The Intelligent Investor* (Harper & Row, 1973), is recognized for having articulated reasoned investment principles for the individual investor. It is helpful to see the investment process from Dodd's perspective, especially when comparing the effort and attention an investor must expend to achieve certain outcomes.

Dodd separates investors into two categories. *Defensive investors* emphasize avoidance of serious mistakes, as well as freedom from "effort, annoyance, and the need for making frequent decisions." In contrast, *enterprising* or *aggressive investors* are willing to devote time and care to the selection of securities that are both sound and more attractive than the average. The expectation is that the aggressive investor is able to outperform the defensive investor, due to the extra time and effort devoted to the enterprise. Dodd doubted this premise would be true in all types of markets; the speculative technology bubble that burst in April 2000 proved his point. To be truly successful, Dodd suggested, the aggressive investor must make sure his results will not be worse than the defensive investor's.

Another expectation is that all you have to do is find the best company within an industry sector that is itself most likely to grow in the future. The problem here, challenges Dodd, is this "is not as easy as it always looks in retrospect." Dodd concludes that "obvious prospects for physical growth in a business do not translate into profits for investors." Even experts have no "dependable ways of selecting and concentrating on the most promising companies in the most promising industries."

I find that Dodd's insights are quite accurate. If you think of the effort that it takes to screen, select, and manage a large number of individual stocks, there better be a payoff in terms of higher profits than can be achieved with less activity. That brings us to the question of what you should be shooting for.

Beating the Market

When structuring the growth portion of a portfolio, one of the first questions to ask is, are you trying to beat the market?

If the answer is yes, then the risk level of the portfolio needs to be raised through concentration, leverage, trading, or some other enhancement technique. To do that, you need to be well versed in the markets, have money that you can afford to lose, and be skilled not only in selecting and monitoring your investments, but also in taking profits and cutting losses. Most people reading this book probably do not fall into this category of investor.

If the answer is no, then it is much wiser to use diversified pools such as index mutual funds or exchange traded funds that replicate the market. If you are trying to enhance performance in a downward or sideways market, managed mutual funds are appropriate and, if well chosen, can be expected to outperform the indexes at those times.

Results

As Warren Buffett said of performance in the 1998 annual report for Berkshire Hathaway:

> Given our gain of 34.1%, it is tempting to declare victory and move on. But last year's performance was no great triumph: *Any* investor can chalk up large returns when stocks soar, as they did in 1997. In a bull market, one must avoid the error of the preening duck that quacks boastfully after a torrential rainstorm, thinking that its paddling skills have caused it to rise in the world. A right-thinking duck would instead compare its position after the downpour to that of the other ducks on the pond.
>
> So what's our duck rating for 1997? . . . though we paddled furiously last year, passive ducks that simply invested in the S&P Index rose almost as fast as we did. Our appraisal of 1997's performance, then: Quack.

Summary

There are many ways to approach stock investing, some of which will have more appeal to you than others due to your own personal preferences and the amount of time you want to commit to the effort. Even the most respected of stock investors know their limitations.

CHAPTER 13

Selecting Investments for Capital Appreciation

How do you begin the process of choosing investments that meet your growth objectives? Some investors rely on the advice of their portfolio managers and stockbrokers, who in turn rely on research. Portfolio managers generally use research published by the brokerage firms that place their trades or they may purchase research from independent research houses.

Brokers usually rely on the research published by the companies that employ them. Many times the research is condensed into a "focus list," which is a short list of recommended stocks. In-house research grew dramatically after brokerage firms realized they needed to add value when competing for clients, especially after the 1975 deregulation of securities commissions and the advent of discount brokerage. Discount brokerage firms do not hire their own analysts. Instead, they usually provide their clients with independently published research.

Individuals investing on their own may be familiar with such publications as *Value Line* and *Morningstar*, which are published by research houses that have no connections with underwriting or sales functions. Both are available at public libraries and by subscription in print and software. (Morningstar information is also available on the Internet for free or on a subscription basis.) Value Line, started by

Arnold Bernhard in 1931 specifically for the individual investor, is probably the oldest independent source of stock research. You may be familiar with Morningstar as a publisher of a mutual fund publication. It has recently started following stocks as well. In this chapter, we consider how to compare stocks with the view of understanding which stocks you would like to own, using sources that are readily available to you through your local library or online.

Categories of Stocks

To put your stock choices in context, it helps to differentiate them by grouping them by category. While there are numerous ways to do this, let's use the system in Morningstar publications, which is based on financial criteria as well as Morningstar's assessment of the company in issue. While classifications alone will not tell you what to buy, understanding them has two benefits. First, the groupings will assist you in comparing the stocks you are considering to other similar stocks. Second, they will help you assess stocks for diversification and risk purposes.

Morningstar provides data and research reports on over 7,000 stocks. The stocks are screened using Morningstar's proprietary algorithm and grouped in accordance with their underlying fundamentals into one of 8 *types*, 10 *sectors*, and about 100 *industries*. As I review these groupings, some will not appeal to you as an investor, while others might. For example, you may not be interested in Distressed stocks because to benefit from them you would need to wait for a turnaround situation. On the other hand, you may be interested in Classic Growth stocks, which are the type of stock Warren Buffett might favor. Or, you might be interested in the Aggressive Growth type, which shows more "maturity" than Speculative Growth companies, and possibly more potential for capital appreciation than Classic Growth companies.

Types

First, Morningstar screens its database for companies that are in trouble and places them in the "Distressed" type. These are companies with "serious operating problems . . . which could mean declining cash flow, negative earnings, high debt" or a combination of these factors. Stocks that fall into Morningstar's Distressed type are "highly risky," since signs of distress could signal the company may go out of business. Bethlehem Steel and Rite Aid are examples of Morningstar's Distressed stock type. An investor wanting to buy a Distressed stock would have to believe it was going to turn around. Most readers would probably exclude Distressed stocks from their "buy lists." Morningstar excludes "very rapidly growing companies" from this type but includes them under "speculative growth," to be discussed.

Next, Morningstar checks the remaining stocks that it follows and screens for high dividend paying stocks, which it types "High Yield." These would be stocks that pay a dividend that is more than twice the average dividend for large-cap stocks, partly because the company is paying out earnings instead of putting them to work. High Yield stocks might appeal to investors who want to receive dividend income and participate in slow growth at the same time. AT&T, Bank of America, and Eastman Kodak are a few current Morningstar High Yield stocks. Excluded from this type are limited partnerships and real estate investment trusts (REITs), as well as Hard Assets, which are a separate type.

> **◣NOTE◢**
>
> The term **Hard Assets** refers to companies that own or exploit real estate, metals, timber, and other assets with a low correlation to the overall stock market.

Then, Morningstar screens the remaining stocks for the following industries: precious metals, oil and gas, REITs, and other real estate companies. These fall under the Hard Asset type, representing companies that have a below-average correlation to the overall stock market, which would make them suitable for diversification purposes according to Morningstar. Current examples of Hard Asset types are Homestake Mining, Texaco, and Chevron.

Next, Morningstar screens for the Cyclical type—industrial cyclical and consumer durable stocks, which are companies whose profits are likely to be influenced by the overall direction of the economy. Current examples are Corning, Kimberly-Clark, and General Electric.

The remaining stocks fall into the Growth type, which itself is split into four subtypes, Speculative Growth, Aggressive Growth, Classic Growth, and Slow Growth. Speculative Growth is stocks with rapid revenue growth but slow or nonexistent earnings growth. These are companies that tend to be in the early phase of their growth cycle. At best, profits are spotty and at worst, they are nonexistent, according to Morningstar. Currently, Morningstar places Palm, General Motors, and Nextel Communications in the Speculative Growth type.

Aggressive Growth are companies with rapid sales and rapid earnings growth, such as Nokia, Dell Computers, Qualcomm, and Bed Bath and Beyond. Classic Growth are companies with good earnings growth over the long term (at least 3 years) and either good dividend growth over the trailing five years or a dividend yield that is between one half to two times the average for large-cap stocks. Examples are Cigna, Target, and Morgan Stanley Dean Witter.

Slow Growth are companies with slow revenue growth, defined as less than gross domestic product (GDP) growth, and slow earnings growth, defined as less than two times GDP growth. Examples are Dun & Bradstreet and Pathmark stores.

Sectors

Another common way to group stocks is by sector. If you use Morningstar, you will see all the stocks grouped into 10 sectors based on NAICS (North American Industry Classification System) codes, which are used by the U.S. Office of Budget and Management to classify companies according to their businesses. (NAICS codes replace SIC or Standard Industry Classification codes, which had been in use since the 1930s.) The 10 sectors are consumer durables, consumer staples, energy, financials, health, industrial cyclicals, retail, services, technology, and utilities.

Industry

The next level of grouping is by industry, which is the company's primary business description. Morningstar determines industry from the company's business description in the company's Form 10-k, which is filed with the Securities and Exchange Commission (SEC). The over 7,000 stocks Morningstar follows are grouped into about 100 industries.

Market Cap

Morningstar also provides data on market capitalization, or *market cap*, which helps further distinguish stocks. Market cap is calculated by multiplying the current share price by the number of shares out-standing. Morningstar's capitalization is tied to market movement, so that the top 5 percent of all stocks in market capitalization are large caps representing stocks with $5 billion in market capitaliza-tion or above. The next 15 percent are mid-cap (representing $1 bil-lion to $5 billion in market cap) and the remaining 80 percent are small-cap ($1 billion or less).

Examples Morningstar ranks as large-cap stocks are General Elec-tric ($475 billion as of the end of 2000), Exxon Mobil ($30 billion), Pfizer ($29 billion), Cisco Systems ($27 billion), Wal-Mart Stores ($23 billion), and Microsoft ($23 billion). Examples of mid-caps are Adaptec ($1 billion), Tyson Foods, and JCPenney (both $2.8 billion). Examples of small caps are Pier One Imports ($996 million) and Olin ($989 million). The market capitalization for the smallest of the small caps includes Mortgage.com ($1.4 million) and Objectsoft ($200,000) and Home Security International ($300,000).

Valuation

Morningstar also screens its database for valuation and categorizes each stock as "value," "growth," and "blend." The valuation is based on a stock's "P/E" (price-to-earnings ratio) and "P/B" (price-to-book ratio) and compared to the median P/E and P/B of the all the stocks within its market capitalization group. P/B is stock price compared to book value, which is the breakup value of the company. Then, Morningstar scores the stocks and assigns a value, growth, or blend valuation to give you another means of differentiating stocks. This information is useful for diversification purposes.

Subjective Measures

To help individual investors screen for stocks, Morningstar grades stocks based on growth and profitability against other stocks in its sector, as well as general financial health and an evaluation of pre-dictability of stock price. An investor could screen for high grades in each of these categories to arrive at a possible list of stock to con-sider. For example, you screen for B or better as a starting point and then refine your search from there.

Summary

You can look at individual stocks in many different ways when you are assessing which stocks you may wish to purchase. The approach described in this chapter is just of several possibilities. In Chapter 14, I introduce you to Value Line's approach to stock selection and explain how you can use its services to craft an investment policy for yourself that includes when to sell.

Selling Rules and Selection Criteria

Irrespective of the type of instrument you are buying to meet your investment objectives, you need to know how to take two types of actions: when to buy and when to sell. It is easier to buy than to sell, and in fact, many people avoid selling because they have not developed their selling skills. In this chapter, I introduce concepts for you to consider in developing your own selling discipline, which is a very individual and personal exercise. There is probably no other aspect of investing that is more affected by the personality and character of the individual. Even professional money managers differ in how they approach selling rules. There are no universal standards or hard-and-fast rules. At the end of the chapter, I provide an example of an investment policy statement that incorporates selling rules based on selection criteria, using a Value Line selection screen. Selling rules for mutual funds are somewhat different from selling rules for stocks, and are covered in Chapter 15. Selling rules for bonds and money markets are covered in Chapters 16 and 17, respectively.

A selling discipline is a plan of action you have in place *before you buy an investment* that defines the circumstances under which you will sell the investment. Having a selling discipline distinguishes serious investors from people who see the stock market as a game. It is the single most important skill to have if you are investing your own money after 50, particularly if you are investing irreplaceable assets.

In this chapter I develop the concept of a selling discipline with stocks. In later chapters I contrast rules that would apply to other types of instruments, including stock mutual funds and fixed income investments.

Background

"Buy low and sell high" is actually a simple selling rule. The concept underlying the rule is a good one: To make a profit in a stock, you have to sell at a higher price than you paid to buy the stock. Beyond that, the rule is useless to an investor and in fact may be harmful. It implies you have to buy a stock when it is down, which may not work for you unless you are a value investor, you have correctly assessed the fundamentals of the stock, and you are willing to see the stock go down in price because you hope it will turn around some day in the future. Moreover, it gives you a false sense of security that you actually have a selling discipline.

NOTE

A selling discipline is a plan of action you have in place before you buy an investment that defines the circumstances under which you will sell the investment.

"Sell your losers and let your profits ride" is an improvement over the first rule. Since you need to sell at a profit to make money, this rule tells you your goal without implying that you need to buy undervalued stocks. It adds another element, that of selling off losing positions. Here you have a sense of the two essential elements of an effective selling rule: To make money, you must not only take advantage of rising stock prices, but also protect your assets by selling off those positions that put you in jeopardy. A further refinement is "Cut your losses and take your profits."

However, both these rules fall short of what you need to develop for yourself because they don't spell out exactly what will happen after you buy a stock. Let's take a different type of rule that sets a selling point.

Stop Loss

One popular selling rule is to limit losses at some percentage point below the purchase price. That is, the investor chooses to limit the loss on a stock at some arbitrary stop loss, usually 10 percent below the purchase price or cost basis. I call this type of selling rule a *basis stop loss* because it is calculated off your cost basis. For example, you buy a stock at $100 a share. If the stock drops to $90 a share, you sell. This type of selling rule helps protect you from serious losses if you apply it religiously to each of your individual stocks. Theoretically, if executed properly, the basis stop loss limits your losses to 10 percent of your overall stock portfolio at any point in time.

Say you bought a certain technology stock on January 6, 2000, at $30 a share. Applying the basis stop loss at 10 percent, you sold 10 months later in October at $27 a share. Selling at that time would have successfully protected you from a loss of 40 percent had you held on another few months. If you had bought 1,000 shares in January for $30,000, you would have successfully limited your loss to $3,000 instead of losing $12,000 a few months later.

The basis stop loss is a big improvement over a fuzzy rule such as "buy low and sell high" since it actually tells you when to get out. But, it does not go far enough because it misses the other side of the coin, profit taking. Remember that the purpose of a selling discipline is not just to protect your downside, but also to take a profit.

> **TIP**
>
> Cut losses with a basis sell stop and take profits with a rising stop.

Rising Stop

Between January and October 2000, the technology stock rose from $30 to $88. If you had sold at that time, your $30,000 investment in January would have more than doubled to $88,000, a profit of $58,000. If you were working solely with a selling rule to protect your downside exposure as discussed earlier, you would have sold your position when you reached your basis stop loss. But, you would have lost the opportunity to make over $50,000. Your selling rule needs to help you enter a selling order even if you are not worried at the time about losing your original investment due to the unrealized profit you see in the stock.

One way to structure a profit-taking selling rule is to continue to raise your stop loss as the price of the stock rises. That would change the basis stop loss into a rising stop that floats with rising stock prices, which I like to think of as a *profit point* instead of a stop loss. Adopting these concepts, you might state your selling rule as "Cut losses with a basis sell stop and take profits with a rising stop." This gives you a basic framework on which to build a selling discipline.

If you had been working with this technology stock, your basis stop loss would have been $27, which is essentially the lowest price at which you were willing to own the stock. The basis stop is easy. Setting the rising stop is harder, since you have to keep adjusting it if the stock is actually going up in price. In the case of the technology stock in this example, you could have adjusted the rising stop any number of times during the 10 months the stock rose to a high of $88. To make things easier for themselves, some people sell off some of their profits at arbitrary profit points of 10 percent or 25 percent above the purchase price. The disadvantage of doing that is selling out before a big move in a stock. How you set up your own system will depend on how much time you devote to investing and whether you are working alone or with a broker or adviser.

Practical Application

None of this discussion will be of any value unless you can actually come up with a system that works for you. Whether you are working alone or with a stockbroker or adviser, you need to devise something you can manage. It takes some thought about what you are trying to achieve, how often you monitor your stocks, and how much time you have to focus on these issues on a regular basis. Part of the time commitment depends on how you select stocks and how much risk you are taking on.

Risk

If you are investing aggressively, you need to look at your stocks more frequently than if you are investing conservatively. High-risk stocks generally tend to have wider price swings and deeper lows than low-risk stocks with stronger fundamentals. If you trade aggressively, you need a stronger selling discipline, unless you are just playing the market as a form of entertainment.

If you don't sell a stock when you need to, you can convince yourself that you are making money when you aren't. You can just tell yourself your losers will recover—some day. In fact, you may play the game of changing your horizon on a stock from short term to long term, just to avoid admitting a mistake. Selling takes courage and conviction and so does having the sense to know you need to bring some discipline to your investing.

Stock Selection

As discussed in Chapter 8, selling rules are part of an overall investment policy. They are best set at the same time you determine your selection criteria since you want to sell when a stock falls out of favor. What I mean is that you need to deselect a stock (sell it) when you determine that it no longer passes your selection criteria.

Many, if not most, professional money managers work with a written investment objective to guide the portfolio and a written investment policy statement to execute and manage it. The policy might contain deselection criteria, as well as management issues such as whether the portfolio will be leveraged, diversified, or concentrated, and the like. Most importantly, it states the selection criteria, which automatically guides the manager in terms of deselection; that is, when a stock is no longer suitable to buy, it is also not suitable to hold and must be sold.

Value Line

In this section, I explain how a possible investment policy can be structured using Value Line as a resource. First, let's review how Value Line rankings work.

Value Line's print publication reports on about 90 industries and 1,700 stocks and ranks both for purchase criteria, such as timeliness, safety, and technical rankings. The software version reports on 6,000 stocks. These rankings are based on different fundamental and technical conclusions the Value Line analysts draw about the stocks and are a form of future assessment of how the stock will do over time. As such, they can be helpful but should not be the sole reason for a purchase. According to Value Line, its highest ranked stocks have outperformed its lowest ranked stocks for over 30 years.

Let me describe the rankings first, and then, let's discuss how you might use them. Timeliness is Value Line's proprietary assessment of the expected price performance of a stock or industry over the next 6 to 12 months. Value Line determines stock timelines based on relative earnings and price growth over the prior 10 years, and to a lesser extent, price momentum, quarterly earnings performance, and earnings surprises. The top 100 stocks are ranked highest (timeliness rank of 1) for expected relative performance over the next 12 months; 300 stocks are ranked 2 (above average); 900 are ranked 3 for average; 300 are ranked 4 for below average; and 100 are ranked 5 for lowest. Stocks ranked 1 and 2 are expected by Value Line to perform better than the rest, but are also more volatile than the rest. Those ranked 4 or 5 have underperformed 1, 2, and 3 ranks in the past, and Value Line expects them to underperform in the future.

Value Line also ranks stocks according to Safety, with a rank of 1 expected to be the safest, that is, the least volatile and most financially strong, and a rank of 5 being the least safe. Two additional Value Line rankings are the Technical Rank and the Income Rank. The Technical Rank, which is ranked 1 (highest) to 5 (lowest), based on an analysis of the stock's relative performance during the prior 52 weeks, projects the stock's expected price performance relative to the overall market over the next three to six months. The Technical Rank would be useful to an investor with a short-term horizon and is best used in concert with the Timeliness and Safety Rank.

Value Line also projects a company's sales, earning, dividends, and other measures over a three- to five-year period. The service also ranks industries for timeliness, as well as individual stocks within those industries.

Sample Investment Policy

Here is an example of a selection strategy using Value Line rankings. This is not a recommendation, but merely illustrates a policy you could create using a tool such as Value Line. This also serves as an example of a simply constructed investment policy statement that can guide your actions as an investor and take some of the mystery out of when to buy and when to sell.

Investment Policy Statement

Objective: Aggressive growth.

Diversification: 10 to 12 stocks in six or more industries.

Leverage: None. Cash account (not margin).

Industry: Timeliness Rank of 1 to 3.

Stocks: Timeliness Rank of 1; Safety Rank of 1 or 2; Technical Rank of 1 or 2.

Deselection criteria: Sell when Timeliness, Safety, or Technical rankings fall. Sell when a stock reaches a basis stop loss. Sell when a stock reaches a rising stop loss.

Summary

When coming up with your own investment policy, you want to consider when to place an order to buy or sell as well as when you will look at the portfolio to make your buy and sell determinations; whether to leverage or enhance the portfolio; and if you are using margin, options, or futures, how you will control the extra risk you are assuming.

CHAPTER 15

Selecting Stock Mutual Funds

Mutual funds that buy stocks can be appropriate choices for the growth portion of your portfolio. How to select and manage a mutual fund portfolio is a subject that deserves a book of its own. Being limited to a chapter, the most I can do here is point you in the right direction. Let's first discuss how to select mutual funds, and then, how to judge the performance of those funds to determine when to sell.

What Not to Do

It is ever so easy to buy a mutual fund. Funds are sold directly through the mail and through registered representatives you can find even in your bank.

If you don't think through the selection process, you might find yourself buying funds that sound familiar to you or that you find in a magazine article that ranks fund performance. Neither method is wise.

Promotion

The shares of mutual funds are offered for sale (and redemption) on a continuous basis, hence the term, "open end" investment company.

Ongoing sales of mutual fund shares are important because mutual funds offer to buy back, or redeem, shares from shareholders.

Some mutual fund sponsors promote their funds through the print and broadcast media and through direct mail. Those mutual funds that sell directly to investors through the mail want you to send in a check. Others that sell through registered representatives want to establish name recognition so that you will recognize the fund when it is presented to you. My guess is that any well-known mutual fund family has a large publicity or advertising budget. You may not recognize the names of some of the fund families that do not advertise or promote themselves. For example, you may not have heard of the American Funds, managed by Capital Research and Management, even though it is one of the largest and oldest fund families. Name recognition is not a sign of good or bad performance or management; it simply reflects marketing strategy and is not a reason on which to base your selection.

NOTE

A registered representative is a licensed sales representative of a firm that is a registered broker/dealer. His license may be limited to mutual fund sales or he may be licensed to sell other securities as well.

Hot Funds

Neither are "hot fund" stories in the press a good way to select funds. Extraordinary performance will get the attention of the news media and result in television, print, and radio interviews for the manager of the fund. Top-of-the-charts results can dazzle, but is that really what you want? If you follow mutual fund performance, you will see that the most volatile funds occasionally reach into the upper limits of performance, but rarely stay there for any length of time.

There are many examples of great influxes of money coming into funds after extraordinary performance, but the problem is that it can be too late for the new investor to benefit. After reading about the hot funds for 1993, you could have bought a top-performing fund that made an astounding 124 percent when the S&P 500 returned only 10 percent. Say you invested $10,000 in that top fund after you put down the magazine. By the end of 2000, your $10,000 would be worth only $1,022, compared with

NOTE

A mutual fund, also known as an open-end investment company, offers shares to the public on a continuous basis.

$32,310 if you had invested the same amount in an S&P 500 Index fund. Remember this key fact: Performance rankings are based on what other investors experienced, not what you can expect if you invest.

Finding Your Stock Funds

In determining what to look for, keep in mind that you are buying a particular fund for a particular personal investment objective, such as growth of capital. You are choosing that fund because you want to hire the fund's portfolio manager and you have the expectation that he will perform in a certain manner. If you hire a value manager, you do not want to see growth stocks in the portfolio. If you hire a growth manager, you don't want him to buy value stocks, or worse, a large position of bonds.

TIP

Name recognition is not a sign of good or bad performance or management, it simply reflects marketing strategy and is not a reason on which to base your selection.

When considering different types of funds, look for funds that invest in stocks and have investment objectives that relate to growth, capital appreciation, long-term growth, and the like. The investment objectives of a fund drive the investment activity of the fund's portfolio manager. You can find the objective in the fund's prospectus, which is a legal document describing the offering to investors. If you keep in mind that prospectuses would not be written but for investor protection laws, you will want to read every prospectus for every fund you intend to buy. Don't skip the risk section.

Also, be sure to understand how much it costs to (1) buy the fund, (2) own the fund, and (3) sell, or redeem, the fund to get your money out. The cost to buy a fund is the *commission* or *load*, which can be zero. The cost to own the fund is the *total operating expense*, which includes a certain type of fee that is called a *12b-1 fee*, which I discuss later. The cost to sell the fund can be either a *redemption fee* or a *contingent deferred sales charge* (CDSC). The CDSC can be zero or it can decrease over time to zero. All funds have a cost to own. Not all funds charge a fee to buy. Not all funds charge a fee to redeem.

TIP

Remember that performance rankings are based on what other investors experienced, not what you can expect if you invest.

Some people go astray thinking that a smart investor should be buying no-load funds that do not charge a fee to buy the fund. This can backfire on you in a big way. A woman contacted me about a problem she was having with her broker. Jill had sold her house for $800,000 and had given the check to her broker, telling him that she wanted to invest in a no-load mutual fund for up to two years. (Jill's intention was to use that money to buy another house within two years.) The broker obliged by selling her a Class B mutual fund, which had no charge to buy. Not too long after that, Jill needed her money and found out that she could get it back only after a deduction for a contingent deferred sales charge. Jill did not recall the broker mentioning the charge, but it was disclosed in the prospectus, which she had not read.

You do not want to find yourself in this situation, especially if you are investing irreplaceable assets. Remember that if you are buying a fund in person, the registered representative who is working with you needs to get paid, and payment is usually a commission at the time of the sale plus an ongoing 12b-1 fee for the length of time you own the fund. If a fund has a sales charge, however, it is usually lower the more you invest and usually goes to zero over $1 million.

Jill had asked for an investment that paid the broker nothing for his efforts, which was shortsighted of her. And, at the same time, the broker was self-serving. He could have offered a money market mutual fund, which is normally sold with no commission and no charge to redeem, or U.S. Treasury bills or notes (discussed in Chapter 16). Or, he could have offered Class A shares of the same fund instead of Class B shares. The prospectus describes the different classes of shares and their pricing.

By selling the Class B shares to Jill, the broker's commission was about twice as high as he would have made on Class A shares. Plus, his ongoing compensation through 12b-1 fees was also about twice as high. By buying the Class B shares, Jill was paying nothing to buy the shares. But,

Class B shares came with a "penalty" at the time of redemption and owning them cost about twice as much in total operating expenses.

In Jill's case, her penalty came to $40,000 (5% of $800,000) and her operating costs were almost double (1.6% vs. 0.7% per year). If Jill's broker had sold her Class A shares instead, she would have paid a load of 2 percent of $800,000 which comes to $16,000. Depending on his arrangement with his firm, he could have received anywhere from 40 percent to 90 percent of this commission for the Class A shares ($6,400 to $14,400) compared with anywhere from 40 percent to 90 percent of $36,000 for the Class B shares ($14,400 to $32,400). Jill thought she was being smart by asking for a no-load fund. It is smarter to look at overall pricing, ask the broker some tough questions, and read the prospectus before you buy, especially if you are over 50 and investing irreplaceable assets.

Research

Proper selection of mutual funds requires research. Happily, there are fine research publications that make the job much easier than it was just a few years ago. Many of these tools are available online and in your library including Morningstar, Value Line, and Steele Systems, Inc. (see Appendix). Any one of these resources can help you judge the quality of the manager. You may also wish to look at Standard & Poor's Select Fund Bulletin, which you can find online at www.standardandpoors.com/onfunds. The S&P Select Fund Bulletin publishes a short list of screened funds that pass their selection criteria.

I like the publication because the screening methodology embodies my personal preference for selecting funds based on management skill, consistency of performance, and most important, a reasonable expectation that performance will be repeated. This type of fund may not be picked up by the media, because there is no story to tell. Work proceeds on a consistent basis, day in and day out, with the manager following the investment objectives of the fund. Performance is as expected for the category of fund. There is no sizzle. Just performance.

> **NOTE**
> Proper selection of mutual funds requires research. Happily, there are fine research publications that make the job much easier than it was just a few years ago.

When to Sell

After you own a fund, how do you know it is time to sell? Now, you need to look at performance reports and compare your fund with similar funds. After you own the fund, you need to look at performance to determine if there is any reason to sell it.

It is essential to compare similar funds, since you learn nothing about the performance of your aggressive growth fund by comparing it with an intermediate bond fund, or vice versa. There are essentially three types of mutual funds: (1) stock funds, with the objective of growing your capital; (2) bond or fixed-income funds, with the objective of income; and (3) money market funds, for stability of principal. You also can have a hybrid fund that combines stocks and bonds.

You want to compare stock funds with stock funds, bond funds with bond funds, and money market funds with money market funds. In fact, you want to slice even finer. If you own a technology fund, you will not want to compare it with a large cap value fund, even though both are stock funds.

Start with performance figures for the most recent period. Compare your fund with other funds that have the same investment objective and category. Take a particular emerging growth fund offered by a company's 401(k) plan as an example. If I look up the fund in Steele Systems, Inc., I find it is listed as having a small cap growth objective in the aggressive growth category. There were 443 funds in this classification at the end of the year 2000.

> **NOTE**
>
> There are essentially three types of mutual funds: (1) stock funds, with the objective of growing your capital; (2) bond or fixed-income funds, with the objective of income; and (3) money market funds, for stability of principal. You also can have a hybrid fund that combines stocks and bonds.

If you look at performance alone, you may miss something important. In 1999, this fund returned 48 percent, which was more than double the return of the S&P 500 Index. But, if you compare peers, this performance was far less than the average for the group, which was 65 percent for the period. This tells you how important it is to put performance into the context of what the manager is trying to achieve. The fund had a very impressive start in 1994 with a 23 percent return when the group averaged zero, placing it at the very top of the rankings.

Looking further, I see that the fund performed at the bottom of the pool for performance through the year 2000, ranking 413 out of 443.

On a longer term basis, the story is not much better. With average annual returns of 4.5 percent for the past three years compared with an average of 14.3 percent, the fund ranked in the bottom 20 percent for three-year performance. Five-year performance was worse. At 5.2 percent average annual returns, compared with 14.12 percent for the group, the fund ranked 197 out of 212 similar funds in existence for the full five-year period. This fund is not performing as expected and should be replaced.

Summary

Investing in mutual funds is a much easier task for most people than investing in stocks. To help you pick good stock mutual funds, numerous tools are available to you at your library. In selecting stock mutual funds for yourself, don't look for top performers, look for funds that offer performance that is consistent with what they are seeking to achieve. Finding those funds will require some research on your part or the help of a good registered representative or investment adviser who uses mutual funds in his portfolios. Many mutual fund companies that sell directly to investors have excellent Web sites that can help you review different funds for possible purchase. I also recommend you read the fund reviews written by the publications mentioned in the Appendix, but avoid picking funds off a top fund ranking. Sell your funds when they no longer fit your personal investment objectives, or when the fund no longer performs as expected for the type of fund.

TIP

In selecting stock mutual funds for yourself, don't look for top performers. Look for a fund that offers performance consistent with what the fund is seeking to achieve.

CHAPTER 16

Investing for Income

M ost people over 50 have to invest for income at some point in the future. While many people know how to buy stocks for growth, knowing how to turn assets into income is a far less familiar concept. When I first came to Wall Street shortly after graduating from law school, I thought of all investments as having one goal: to make a profit. Investing for "income" was a fuzzy concept until I started writing mutual fund prospectuses, which are legally mandated disclosure documents describing the terms of an offering. Then, I began to understand that total return comprises two components: One measures price movements due to market action; the other measures distributions, such as interest, dividends, or capital gains.

I realized you could separate the two components. You could measure a bond based on how much the bond's principal fluctuated in value over time and you could also measure the bond's interest payments. That made it clear to me that you could use a bond or bond fund to achieve two different objectives. To make a profit, you could buy a bond or bond fund with the intention of selling it at a higher price, much like a growth investment. Or, you could buy a bond and hold onto it until maturity, while receiving interest payments that you could spend, or put another way, use for "income production."

Working on prospectuses forced me to think about different types of instruments of the market in terms of their intended purposes. The managers of the mutual funds who bought these investments for the funds did so for a reason. They sought to achieve a certain result, such as growth of capital, production of income, or preservation of capital. This helped crystallize in my mind the real difference between a growth investment, which you would normally buy to make a profit at the time of sale, versus an income investment, which you might purchase for income production. While some investors do buy stocks and sell them when they want cash for living expenses, the problem with this strategy is that bad stock choices and down markets put your capital at great risk, and if that capital is irreplaceable, you may find yourself having to get a job at the age of 80. A less risky strategy would be to structure your income portfolio around income-producing investments from which you can withdraw distributions instead of selling off principal. You still have to deal with risks, but done correctly, you can avoid selling off principal to meet your cash flow needs, and continue to grow your portfolio with stock investments in the growth portion of your portfolio. (We discussed how to figure the amount of money you should invest in bonds for income production in Chapters 6 and 7.)

> **NOTE**
> A bond has two components, principal and interest. Interest is usually fixed, while principal fluctuates due to market forces.

Bonds

> **NOTE**
> After a bond matures, you could use the proceeds to buy another to continue your income production. Since the interest rate on the new bond will depend on then current interest rates, you will not know exactly how much income to expect beforehand.

Certain financial instruments are designed to pay the investor a certain amount of money (interest) for a certain length of time and to repay the original amount of the investment (principal) at the end of that time (maturity date). Called *fixed income instruments* or *bonds*, they work just like an IOU. The investor is the lender. The borrower (issuer) can be the federal government, the state you live in, your municipality, or a corporation. Thus, you could have U.S. bonds, state bonds, municipal bonds, corporate bonds, and bonds issued for a specific purpose, such as raising money to build a hospital or a road.

If you buy a U.S. government bond, you are actually lending money to the federal government in exchange for two promises: to pay you regular interest payments in accordance with the terms of the bond and to repay the amount the government borrowed from you at the agreed upon time. The bond is the government's IOU promising to pay you back when the loan comes due, plus interest during the time of the loan. You can buy government bonds directly from the Federal Reserve Bank or through your local banker or broker.

Interest Rates

An important element of the IOU is the interest rate, which is usually fixed for the life of the loan ("fixed rate"). If the coupon on your 30-year U.S. bond is 6 percent, the lender, the federal government, agrees to pay you 6 percent per year for 30 years, not more, not less. Some bonds do have variable interest rates and some pay interest only at maturity. At the time you consider purchasing a bond, you need to know the interest rate features and whether they are fixed, or *floating* or *ac-creted*. A floating rate changes over time in accordance with the terms of the bond. Interest is accreted in bonds such as zero-coupon bonds, which are issued at a discount from face value with interest paid only at maturity.

> **NOTE**
>
> The bond is the government's IOU promising to pay you back when the loan comes due, plus interest during the time of the loan.

Another important aspect of an IOU is that the borrower has no obligation to repay you until the maturity date. If you buy a $10,000 30-year U.S. Treasury bond due in the year 2031 and want your money back from the borrower in 2011, you are out of luck. The Federal Reserve Bank has no obligation to repay the loan until 2031. While you won't be able to get your money back from the government before maturity, nothing prevents you from selling the bond to anyone who wants to buy it. Let's talk about how that might work.

Selling Your Bonds

If your next-door neighbor were in the market for a $10,000 20-year U.S government bond, would he buy yours for $10,000? Put yourself in his position. How would you determine a fair price if the bond has a 6 percent yield and 10 years left until maturity? Wouldn't you want to know what kind of interest you could get if you bought a brand-new bond from the Federal Reserve? What if you could get a 10-year bond yielding 12 percent instead of 6 percent?

An investor who could buy a 12 percent U.S. government bond for $10,000 would not pay $10,000 for a 6 percent bond. A $10,000 investment in a 12 percent bond creates $1,200 of interest each year while the same investment in a 6 percent bond pays interest of only $600 a year. To equalize things, you would have to be willing to sell your 6 percent bond at such a price that it would equal the interest payments an investor could get for a 12 percent bond. If the investor gave you $5,000, then his $600 yearly interest payments from the government would equal 12 percent, which is what he can get at the current market. (I have simplified the math in this example and the following one to underscore the concept of how bonds react to market forces due to interest rate changes.) That would mean that if you really needed to cash in your 6 percent bond, you would have to sell it for $5,000 instead of $10,000, a loss of 50 percent of your investment.

NOTE

Another important aspect of an IOU is that the borrower has no obligation to repay you until the maturity date.

Since bond prices and interest rates are inversely related, when interest rates go up, bond prices go down. That's how bond pricing works as shown in the preceding example. Similarly, if interest rates go down, bond prices go up. If interest rates had fallen to 3 percent in this example, you could have sold your bond for $20,000, a 100 percent profit. However, if you had purchased the bond for income purposes, you would have had to use the full $20,000 to buy another bond to replicate your $600-a-year income stream.

You may be thinking that interest rates on U.S. government bonds can't fluctuate all that much, since you don't hear about people losing money if they sell their government bonds before maturity. Let me give you a few historical facts. If you had purchased a 20-year U.S. government bond in October 1972, your coupon would have been 6 percent. If you wanted to sell that bond in February 1980, you would have lost 50 percent of your principal, since bond interest rates had risen to over 12 percent. Similarly, the price of even the highest quality corporate bonds fell more than 50 percent in value in the early 1980s when interest rates rose, meaning that investors who had to sell their bonds would have locked in their losses due to market forces.

Length of Maturity

Fixed income instruments are issued in periods ranging from the very short (under one year) to the very long (30 years or longer). The longer the maturity (and thus the income stream), the greater the impact on price in changing interest rate environments. And, the longer the maturity of the bond, the greater likelihood that interest rates will change during the holding period. That translates into higher risk. The shorter the maturity of the bond, the lower the chance that interest rate fluctuation will impact the bond's market price should you have to sell before maturity.

Creditworthiness

Another element to consider is the borrower's ability to keep its promises to you. An IOU is an unsecured debt, which means there is no collateral you can sell in the event of a default. If you borrow money from a bank to buy a home, the bank has a collateral interest in your home to protect itself if you stop paying the mortgage. That is, the bank has the right to foreclose on the mortgage and sell your house to collect on the loan if you default. In the case of a bond, you are the lender, but you have no collateral to sell if the borrower defaults. All you have is the promise of the borrower to pay you in accordance with the terms of the bond.

U.S. government bonds are backed by the full faith and credit of the United States, which makes them the most creditworthy bonds you can buy. The creditworthiness of the borrower ("issuer") is an important factor to consider when you are lending money by buying a bond because there is no collateral to sell if the issuer defaults on the loan. If you want to get some independent guidance on whether an issuer can make good on its bond promises, you can look at one of the rating services, such as Standard & Poor's (S&P), Moody's Investor Service, Fitch's, or Duff & Phelps. Rating books published by these companies are available in the library and by subscription.

The highest rating assigned for corporate bonds by S&P is AAA, which means the issuer's capacity to pay interest and repay principal is "extremely strong." BBB-rated bonds have "adequate capacity" to pay interest and repay principal. However, "adverse economic conditions or changing circumstances are likely to lead to weakened capacity to pay interest and repay principal." B-rated bonds have the current capacity to pay interest but have "greater vulnerability to default." C-1 is not paying interest currently. Debt rated D is in payment default.

If some borrowers that issue bonds are more likely to pay you interest and repay your principal and others are less likely to do so, why would you ever invest in the latter? People buy the lower rated bonds for one reason, the higher yields. To compete for capital, companies that are less creditworthy need to pay a higher yield to bondholders to attract their interest. Depending on the issue and the market, you may find a difference in yield of 3 or 4 percent between a high rated bond and a low rated bond. If you are trying to generate income from bonds and high-quality bonds are paying say 7 percent and low-quality bonds are paying 10 percent, you may find yourself buying the higher yielding, lower rated bonds. A 3 percent yield spread on a $1 million bond portfolio means an extra $30,000 a year of interest payments.

NOTE

Instead of reinvesting bond fund dividends, you could have them sent to you each month. Or, you could have them invested in your money market mutual fund, which you then could use as a checking account. Or, you could have them sent to your bank account.

As an over-50 investor, however, remember that higher yields always translate to higher risk. Diversification helps lessen risk and managed diversified bond funds may be the answer for many investors over 50 who want higher yield and are willing to take the risk trade-off. Soundly managed higher-yielding bond mutual funds are a good option if the investor wants an income stream and accepts that net asset value or share price will fluctuate. This strategy is not for everyone since you have to know how to judge one mutual fund against another and know when your fund needs to be replaced with another. I would rarely if ever recommend purchasing individual high yield bonds, since the likelihood of default in paying interest as promised or repaying principal when due is inevitably greater for higher yielding bonds. If you are interested, you can find default rates for different periods published by the rating firms referred to earlier. The bonds of some high-yield issuers stop trading since no one wants to buy them. Some companies go out of business.

Redemption or Call Features

Some bonds are issued under an agreement that gives the issuer the right to repay the principal before the maturity date. Known as a call feature, this gives the issuer (who is borrowing money from you) the ability to pay off high interest debt and sell new bonds at lower rates when interest rates fall. The call feature is a benefit to the lender and a detriment to you the investor, since you will be in the position of having to replace the income stream you have been relying on in a lower yielding market. Also, the federal government has from time to time instituted a repurchase or buy-back program to buy back your U.S. government bonds before maturity.

Summary

If you want your investments to generate cash flow for you to live on, you will probably find that bonds are better than stocks for that purpose. Generally, dividends paid by companies on stocks tend to be much lower than interest on bonds. Bonds are also useful to diversify your stock portfolio, as discussed in Chapter 5.

To lessen the risks inherent in purchasing bonds, your most important considerations will be creditworthiness, length of maturity, and call features. There are several ways to lessen risk. First, if you are buying a bond to generate income, buy quality. Second, "ladder" the bonds so that some mature every year or two, which will lessen your exposure to market risk. Third, if you can't afford quality because you need more income than high-quality bonds can give you, be absolutely certain to diversify your bond portfolio with different bonds and maturities or consider diversified bond mutual funds.

> **NOTE**
>
> To lessen the risks inherent in purchasing bonds, your most important considerations will be creditworthiness, length of maturity, and call features.

Finally, some brokers may tell you that you do not need to buy bonds for income purposes. Instead, they believe that you can buy stocks and sell them when you need money to live on. This strategy works only when the stock market is going up, and it can put you out of business very quickly when it is going down.

CHAPTER 17

Investing for Preservation of Capital

Of the three investment purposes we have been discussing—growth, income, and preservation of capital—the last is the least risky. Investments that preserve your capital keep it safe against market losses. Even those with no experience buying stocks, bonds, or mutual funds have opened savings accounts and certificates of deposit (CDs) and bought U.S. savings bonds. When you invest this way you are actually investing for "preservation of capital," not for growth and not for income.

In this chapter, I discuss expectations if you invest for preservation of capital, circumstances in which preservation of capital should and should not be your goal, and the best instruments to use for this purpose. At the end, I point out a popular scam that you should avoid.

No one wants to lose money. Investing for preservation of capital is the safest way to invest. In case you might think that after 50, you should take the least amount of risk with your portfolio and invest everything in instruments that preserve your capital, let me point out why most of you should not. When you invest for preservation of capital, you are protecting your principal against steep declines due to market fluctuations. But, as with any investment, there is a cost to investing this way. The cost is a lower return. Since you are investing for safety, your return will be low on a real basis. *Real return* is your return after accounting for inflation.

Let's explore real return for a moment. In Chapter 3, we discussed market data before and after inflation. We said U.S. Treasury bills, which are money market instruments appropriate for preservation of capital, returned 3.8 percent per year on average. After inflation is taken into account, the return drops to 0.7 percent per year, which is the real inflation-adjusted return. This data, for the period 1929 through 1999, is provided by Ibbotson Associates. (If you also subtracted your income tax liability, this would reduce your real return even further.)

In contrast, the total return on long-term government bonds for the same period was 5.1 percent before inflation and 2.0 percent after in-

flation. The total return on corporate bonds was higher: 5.6 percent before inflation and 2.5 percent after inflation. And, as expected, stock returns were even higher. Stocks of large companies as represented by the S&P 500 Index, returned 11.3 percent per year before inflation for the period 1929 through 1999, and 8 percent in real terms (inflation-adjusted). This comparison underlines the need to consider the risk-reward relationship of different investments before structuring a portfolio after 50—concepts discussed in earlier chapters.

NOTE

When you invest for preservation of capital, you are protecting your principal against steep declines due to market fluctuations.

There are times when assuming the least amount of market risk is an absolute necessity. A widow was referred to me by her insurance agent a few weeks after her husband's sudden death due to a heart attack. The agent had delivered a check to Meg for $1 million, which was the death benefit on her husband's insurance policy. Meg had never invested, and in fact, had never gone to the bank, or even written a check; her husband had closely controlled the finances in the family, leaving Meg totally in the dark. Not surprisingly, Meg was frantic. She had three teenagers to raise alone. And, she had to make financial decisions for herself for the first time in her life. My recommendation to Meg was to invest for preservation of capital for an entire year, by investing the entire $1 million into U.S. Treasury bills. This strategy would allow her to protect her principal from risk of loss and give her time to settle into a routine at home without worrying about losing her money. It would also allow her to learn about the risks and potential rewards of different market instruments at her leisure over the next year, rather than under the pressure of having to make a quick decision that might involve a risk she could not reasonably assess in her current circumstances. Then, after a year, Meg could make better decisions based on her understanding of the risk-reward tradeoffs the market offered her.

There are other times when you might invest for preservation of capital. You may wish to set aside a portion of your overall portfolio for this purpose for emergencies, to stabilize your portfolio, or for a temporary parking place while you assess what you want to do with your money. For emergencies, some recommend setting aside enough to cover six months of living expenses.

Instruments

The financial instruments of the market that are most suited for preservation of capital are money market instruments, which are short-term (under one year) debt instruments. Debt instruments are IOUs, as discussed in Chapter 16. Money market instruments are not expected to fluctuate in price due to market conditions, in part due to their short maturity, or due to how they are structured. For example, if you buy a 1-year certificate of deposit, by definition, you will get your original investment at the end of the holding period irrespective of interest rate changes or market action. You will also get your agreed-on interest payment. Another example is a money market mutual fund, which allows your principal to remain stable, with only the dividend fluctuating in response to interest rates. U.S. Treasury bills are also money market instruments; however, unlike CDs or money market mutual funds, the price of Treasury bills does fluctuate with interest rates. The shorter the maturity, the less likely the impact of price fluctuations. For example, a 3-month bill will be less volatile than a 12-month bill if interest rates change. If you intend to buy a bill and to hold onto it until it matures, the fluctuation will not affect you in any way. When you buy a Treasury bill, you pay less than the face value (par) and your interest is "accreted," meaning you get the interest when you redeem the bill. The difference between the purchase price and the amount you get at maturity is the interest you earn on the bill. You can buy U.S. Treasury bills directly from the Federal Reserve Bank. You can do this by mail or online at www.treasurydirect.gov.

> **TIP**
>
> For emergencies, some recommend setting aside enough to cover six months of living expenses.

As discussed earlier, money market instruments generally do not pay distributions (interest or dividends) that are much higher than the current rate of inflation. From time to time, money market rates may seem high. If you were saving in the early 1980s, you might have put your money into CDs or money market mutual funds. At the time, you could have earned 13 or 15 percent per year or more. And, you could have purchased a 13 or 14 percent 20-year Treasury bond, which was the longest maturity available at the time. When CDs and U.S. Treasury bills earned interest of 13, 14, and even 17 percent per year during 1980 and 1981, the Consumer Price Index (CPI), which measures inflation, was 12 and 13 percent. If you wanted to get a 30-year mortgage to buy a home at this time, you would have had to pay interest in the 12 percent to 18 percent range. Remember to keep that in perspective.

Scams

One of the scams I have come across was brought to me by a lawyer, who received a solicitation, typed on fine letterhead, ostensibly from a large overseas bank. He was ready to send a large amount of money oversees based on a letter he had received from someone he did not know, in exchange for the promise of an extraordinary interest rate. This type of scam was later covered in the press. The lesson here is if it's too good to be true, it probably is.

Summary

Preservation of capital is a valid investment purpose for different times of your life after 50, for at least a part of your portfolio. It can be a valid purpose for your entire portfolio under certain circumstances, for example, when you need to sit on the sidelines for a while or when you have no need to grow your assets or produce any income from your assets for living expenses.

CHAPTER 18

Types of Advisers

Because there is such a confusing array of possibilities, finding the right person to work with is not as easy as it should be. The financial services industry bestows trappings and titles on all levels of personnel. You need to look behind the curtain to see what makes the wizard work. It helps to start with an understanding of how different *advisers*, a term I use as a catchall, are regulated and paid.

Regulation

Regulation exacts accountability. The regulators set certain standards of doing business and impose penalties if the standards are not met. Regulators can suspend a license, charge monetary fines, shut down the adviser's business, and bar him from working in the field.

There are advisers who are regulated by the federal government, others who are regulated by the states, and still others who are not regulated at all. Financial planners, registered investment advisers (including money managers), stockbrokers, and insurance agents are among the advisers who may offer services to you.

Financial Planners

There is no regulation of financial planners as such. Anyone who wants to become a financial planner can do so by putting up a financial planning shingle. Some financial planners voluntarily enroll in educational and certification programs. The Certified Financial Planner Board of Standards is a professional organization that tests and certifies over 30,000 financial planners in the United States, hence the title "Certified Financial Planner" (CFP).

NOTE

Regulators can suspend a license, charge monetary fines, shut down the adviser's business, and bar him from working in the field.

Certification does not mean regulation, however. The Board can revoke a CFP designation, but it cannot put someone out of business. A financial planner may engage in an activity that *does* subject him or her to regulation. Regulated activities are offering investment advice, selling investments, and selling insurance.

Investment Advisers

Generally, anyone offering investment advice for a fee must comply with the federal and state laws governing investment advisers. It is the function, not the title that determines registration requirements. Money managers and portfolio managers fall under this regulatory category, as do some financial planners, and accountants. Whether the investment adviser must register with the U.S. Securities and Exchange Commission (SEC) or a state agency depends on the type and size of his practice. The SEC is the federal governmental agency that governs the regulation of investment advisers. The SEC and the states have the power to censure and fine registered advisers who fail to comply with the law, and to put them out of business.

CAUTION

Anyone who wants to become a financial planner can do so by putting up a financial planning shingle.

The SEC regulates over 8,000 investment advisers, representing about 95 percent of the assets managed by advisers. More than twice as many investment advisers are regulated by the securities commissions of the states in which they do business, according to the North American Securities Administrators Association.

Stockbrokers

Generally, anyone selling stocks, bonds, and other securities falls under the regulatory reach of the federal and state securities laws, as well as the National Association of Securities Dealers (NASD) and in some cases, the New York Stock Exchange. He must be licensed as a registered representative of a registered broker/dealer—an RR for short.

An RR may present himself to you as a financial adviser, financial consultant, account executive, investment professional, or the like. Over time, as the RR increases his sales, he may receive the title of Vice President-Investments and later Senior Vice President-Investments in recognition of his financial contribution to the firm.

The RR may work as an employee of a large Wall Street brokerage firm whose name you would recognize. He may sit in the lobby of your local bank. He may be an employee of a local financial planning firm that has an arrangement with a broker/dealer specializing in recruiting outside salespeople through national advertising. In some states, he may be a CPA with your local accounting firm.

The RR's license may be limited to selling mutual funds and variable annuities. This license is called a *Series 6*. Or it may be a broad license to sell stocks and bonds and other securities in addition to mutual funds and annuities. This broader license is called a *Series 7*. You may also come across Series 63 and Series 24 licenses, which are supervisory in nature. Someone with supervisory responsibility over Series 6 RRs has a Series 63 license in addition to a Series 6 or 7. A person who supervises Series 7 RRs has a Series 24 license in addition to a Series 7.

> **NOTE**
>
> The SEC is the federal governmental agency that governs the regulation of investment advisers. A discretionary manager with over $25 million in assets registers with the SEC. A dually registered nondiscretionary manager with the same assets may be registered locally in the states where they do business, instead of the SEC. A small discretionary manager would also register in the state.

There are over half a million registered representatives in the United States, according to the National Association of Securities Dealers. The NASD is the regulatory body that tests and registers stockbrokers and handles customer complaints filed against them. According to the NASD, 5,156 complaints were filed by customers in 1998. The association barred 369 registered representatives from the securities industry in 1998 and suspended 264 from doing business as RRs.

Insurance Agents

Generally, anyone selling insurance needs to be licensed by the state insurance department in which he is doing business. Most states require the agent to pass a licensing examination and to fulfill continuing education requirements. States have the power to put an agent out of business for failure to comply with the laws governing insurance sales. In some states, your accountant may be licensed to sell insurance. Many stockbrokers have insurance licenses. Mutual fund salespeople with offices in bank lobbies are often insurance licensed. Likewise, it is not unusual for an insurance agent to be licensed to sell mutual funds as well.

How different advisers are paid will also tell you something about what to expect in terms of service.

Commissioned Sales

Whether they are sitting in a major Wall Street firm, the lobby of a bank, a local office building, or in your accountant's office, stockbrokers, insurance agents, and other commissioned salespeople are paid when they make a sale.

CAUTION

Some of these payments to the broker are not disclosed to the client, so it is up to you to ask. The firm's copy of your brokerage statement contains a running total of what your account earns the firm, but your copy does not.

Historically, brokerage firms acted as middlemen to execute stock and bond trades for clients who the broker represented to the firm. As brokerage firms began to manufacture proprietary products, they started requiring brokers to "gather assets." Over time, the broker has evolved from being a "customer's man" to being a salesperson who represents the firm's products and services to the client.

Brokers are paid on commission for agency transactions such as stock purchase and sales. They are paid based on a markup or markdown on principal transactions such as Nasdaq stocks and corporate bonds. They are paid sales credits for the firm's initial public offerings (IPOs), the firm's unit trusts, and the firm's mutual funds. In addition, brokers are paid on their money line, which is a percentage of the assets in your brokerage account.

Some of these payments to the broker are not disclosed to the client, so it is up to you to ask. The firm's copy of your brokerage statement contains a running total of what your account earns the firm, but your copy does not. The firm provides its successful brokers with incentives and awards. In fact, commissioned salespeople are selected and rewarded for their sales ability.

As the client, you have to understand that this is the name of the game. You have to manage the relationship and determine whether the advice you receive is in your best interests or the best interests of the salesperson.

Another factor to be aware of is your need for planning. Many times, commissioned salespeople offer people in your position free retirement planning advice. You need to understand that the longer you take free planning advice, the more beholden you will be to buy something. That is another aspect of the sales process.

And, beware of cold callers. It doesn't happen often, but from time to time, unsophisticated people of retirement age fall prey to high-pressure cold callers working for poorly capitalized firms. Avoid engaging in a conversation with someone who calls you about your investments. It's best for you to take the initiative in finding the right financial adviser instead of reacting to a sales call.

Fees Based on Assets

You will probably come across two types of services for which you would be charged a percentage of assets—the wrap account and the managed portfolio.

WRAP ACCOUNT

A stockbroker may offer you the services of a portfolio manager through the brokerage firm. Called a Managed Account or Wrap Account, the broker introduces a money manager to the client, and the brokerage firm executes the trades and acts as the custodian of the assets. The client pays a wrap fee that includes compensation to the broker, money management fees to the adviser, and the costs of the trades. The wrap fee can be as high as 3 percent of assets per year.

MANAGED PORTFOLIO

A portfolio manager who works for a money management firm is another option. For example, you may be referred to a manager of an aggressive growth portfolio that beat the DOW three years in a row. The firm pays the manager a salary plus a performance bonus.

This type of account is managed by the advisory firm, but the investments maybe held at a brokerage firm. The client pays the brokerage firm commissions, markups, and fees for trades directly out of the account.

The firm charges an additional fee for its services, based on assets in the account. According to industry sources, advisory fees range from 0.75 percent to 3 percent of assets. At $1 million of assets, you can find a portfolio manager who would charge around 1 percent of assets. As is the custom, the portfolio manager's performance figures used to illustrate his past performance do not net out fees. Portfolio managers typically have a minimum account size, with some as high as $20 million, and others as low as $100,000.

> **CAUTION**
>
> As is the custom, the portfolio manager's performance figures used to illustrate his past performance do not net out fees.

If you were to go this route, you would be buying the hope of repeating the performance previously achieved by the portfolio manager. Remember that portfolio managers come in all types, from aggressive to conservative and everything in between.

Some portfolio managers can also set up customized portfolios to meet the particular needs of the client; this is the type of service my firm provides. In those cases, the client is not buying the portfolio manager's past performance. Instead, he is buying the skill of the manager in understanding the client's situation and in customizing a portfolio that meets the individual's ongoing investment needs.

Hourly Billings

You could also be referred to someone who offers retirement planning advice for a fee based on time. The rate charged usually depends on the background and experience of the adviser.

In a consulting arrangement, no investment or product is being sold—but again, because of the variables in this business, this is something you want to confirm. Some sales organizations provide financial planning packages for a nominal fee as a prelude to their goal to gather assets.

In a consulting arrangement, it is important to assess the adviser's skill and knowledge. Ask about background, training, experience, and other clients who the adviser serves. It is important to ask for references and to interview them carefully to determine whether there is a proper fit. In a consulting arrangement, the execution of the advice will have to be done elsewhere.

Summary

Financial advisers usually serve two masters—the client and adviser's firm. The firm may limit the type of advice or investments the adviser may offer because of the way it is regulated or the way it defines its business. As a prospective client, you want to know these limitations before engaging the adviser.

TIP

In a consulting arrangement, it is important to assess the adviser's skill and knowledge.

CHAPTER 19

Interview Rules and Questions to Ask

When you are ready to interview potential advisers, keep the following five rules in mind:

1. As the owner of the assets, you are in charge of the interview, the adviser is not. You are there to get information, to observe, judge, and assess. You are free to ask any questions without embarrassment. And, you are free to end the interview at any time.

2. Your agenda may be different from the adviser's. Be attuned to this possibility. If he is trying to pitch you a product or a service, don't be afraid to cut the interview short.

3. Before you schedule your interviews, make sure you understand your goals and what you want from your adviser. Goals are discussed in Chapters 5, 6, and 7.

4. Understand that some advisers don't give free interviews. You may have to pay for a consultation. The downside is an out-of-pocket cost. The upside is it may remove you from a sales presentation.

5. Don't be too eager to buy something or sign up for a service. Ask for written materials describing services and contracts, if any

NOTE

As the owner of the
assets, you are in
charge of the interview,
the adviser is not.

apply. Ask for a fee schedule. After the interview, read all the materials you receive from the adviser. Talk to references. Take your time.

Questions to Ask at the Interview

When you meet with potential candidates, you are trying to assess skill as well as ability to understand your mission and meet your goals.

Here are four essential open-ended questions to ask advisers offering money management services.

1. *How would you handle my account?* With this question, you are looking for clues on how the adviser defines his business, whether your problem is one he has seen before and can solve, and how he would approach the task. To give you a good answer, he has to understand your goals. Beware if he offers a solution too quickly. Listen for clues about the adviser's expertise and skill and approach. Does he spend time assessing your holdings and goals, does he do a cash flow analysis, does he monitor regularly, does he have a selling discipline? Listen and observe.

    Different advisers have different strengths and weaknesses. Some consider themselves expert stock pickers. Some are fixed income experts. Some stick to insurance products. Some manage aggressive growth portfolios. Get a feel for whether there is a proper fit with your particular needs.

2. *Tell me about some of your other clients who have goals similar to mine and explain how you handle their accounts.* You want to hear the adviser describe a few similar situations. Based on the description, you can judge the adviser's familiarity with the type of problem you need him to solve for you. This should also give you an idea of the types of investment vehicles he would use in your portfolio.

    These are the people you will want to call for a reference, assuming you think the adviser may be a good choice for you. The adviser should be happy to give you names and phone numbers of two or three clients. When you call them, ask open-ended questions about the service. Specific questions about their personal finances would be off limits, of course. As a courtesy, let the adviser know the results of your calls. Also let the adviser know if you did not connect.

3. *Tell me about your background.* The purpose of this question is to understand whom you are dealing with and to try to assess skill. Listen for how the adviser is regulated. Ask for materials that describe his background.

People in the financial services industry come from all kinds of backgrounds. You may be talking to an engineer who decided to become a financial planner two years ago due to a career-ending experience. You may be talking to a successful luxury automobile salesperson who was recruited as a stockbroker. An unrelated background doesn't necessarily mean you won't get good service. But it gives you something to explore further and evaluate in light of the backgrounds and services of other advisers you will be interviewing.

When probing about background, also ask about customer complaints. This is a fair question. You want to know if complaints are a problem.

4. *How will you get paid?* Notice the question is not, how much do you charge? Remember that some advisers are paid indirectly through product sales. Compensation can affect advice. Taking an extreme example, you may be talking to an adviser who only gets paid if he sells you a certain type of product. You pay nothing when you buy that product. But the adviser gets paid a commission for selling it to you. You would want to know that up front.

> **TIP**
>
> Ask about customer complaints. This is a fair question. You want to know if complaints are a problem.

If an adviser is uneasy talking about this subject, that would be enough for me to go elsewhere. Full disclosure of fees you pay and compensation he receives helps maintain an arm's-length relationship, which is an absolute must. It helps you understand if there are any reasons a particular product or service is being recommended over any other.

Here is a list of 12 questions to ask at the time of a particular investment recommendation. I suggest using this checklist *after* you hear the adviser's presentation but *before buying.* Do not skip any questions:

1. Please explain why you are recommending this investment to me.

2. Please explain how the investment meets my objectives.

3. If you have considered alternatives, what are they?

4. If I buy this investment, how much do you get paid at the time I make the investment? How much do you get paid after the purchase (on-going fees)? I would like to see that in writing.

NOTE
Full disclosure of fees you pay and compensation he or she receives helps maintain an arm's-length relationship, which is an absolute must.

5. What are the risks of this investment? I would like to see that in writing (prospectus).

6. How much can I lose?

7. What can I expect to make?

8. What are the penalties or fees, if any, to liquidate the investment? I would like to see that in writing.

9. Is this investment sold by prospectus? I would like to have a copy and read it before making any decisions.

10. How much will it cost me to buy this investment?

11. How much will it cost me to sell?

12. Are any other fees or costs involved?

Summary

If you have any uncertainty about what you are buying, I suggest you go home and write a letter restating your understanding of what you are being offered. Send it to the adviser for a response.

If you are offered an investment that you are told is risk-free, cost-free, and penalty-free, putting that in writing will help clarify matters. If the economist mentioned in Chapter 10, who bought a supposedly risk-free and penalty-free investment, had written such a letter before committing a large amount of money, he would not have made the investment.

CHAPTER 20

Opening a Brokerage Account

M ost stockbrokers are honest, hard-working, and well-trained; they try to do a good job for their clients. Brokerage firms that employ those brokers are required to have established supervisory procedures designed to oversee the activities in your account. It is important to know how to conduct yourself in this environment and to understand what to expect from both the broker and his firm.

Keep in mind, however, that brokers are recruited because of their ability to engender trust, influence the buying decision, and close a sale. Because a broker is a commissioned salesperson, you and your broker have an inherent conflict of interest. That is, your broker will make the most money when your account is active. You will probably make the most money when your account is not traded that frequently. It is because of the potential for the broker to be self-serving that the law has a lot to say about how a broker handles your account. Excessive trading or "churning" is illegal. Unauthorized purchases or sales are illegal. Unsuitable transactions are illegal, and so on. The law is there to protect you for a reason. Chapter 24 discusses illegal practices in more detail.

Cold Callers

When you open your account, it is time to communicate to your broker about investment objectives and how you feel about risk. It is also the time to decide whether you want this person handling your account. Too often, investors only know their brokers over the telephone because a cold caller solicited them and convinced them to purchase an investment product. Other investors are referred through a bank teller to a broker sitting in a bank lobby because the teller noticed a certificate of deposit coming due or a large balance in a checking or savings account. Recently, accountants may become brokers and may approach their accounting clients to become investing clients with them.

There is a better way to find a broker and open an account. That better way is rarely to respond to the cold caller.

Broker of the Day

For now, let's assume you walk into a major Wall Street brokerage firm's office to open an account. If you do not have a contact in mind, the receptionist will steer you to the "broker of the day." The broker of the day could be a rookie or a broker who specializes in options trading, neither of whom is probably right for you. You should tell the receptionist you want to talk to the manager to discuss which of the brokers in the office would be the most suitable person to handle your account.

The Manager

Tell the manager what you want to accomplish with your investment account, what kind of risk you want to take or avoid and ask him to introduce you to an appropriate broker. Have the manager give you his card and tell him you look forward to his supervising your account.

Supervision is a term that has a specific meaning under the law. The branch manager is a supervisor under the law and is held to a high standard of oversight over the broker handling your account. The branch manager is also your first contact should you have a problem with your account.

Interview the broker the manager suggests. As discussed in Chapter 19, look for clues that he understands your needs. Take notes. Get the names of clients you could talk to about his investment style.

Client Agreement

Get copies of the documents you will be asked to sign to open an account and have the broker explain them to you. Pay particular attention to the client agreement and determine if you are agreeing to open a margin account by signing the agreement. While I discuss margin in Chapter 23 in greater detail, for now you need to find out what steps you must take to avoid having your account

"on margin." If you are on margin in your account, the brokerage firm will exercise all its rights to liquidate your account if it feels market conditions jeopardize the firm's capital. You will be notified of a margin call. The firm will expect you to meet the call promptly. They will not listen to your story that the stock will bounce right back. Margin managers are there to observe the rules and protect the firm. Margin is discussed in Chapter 23.

New Account Form

Ask to see the *new account form* the broker will fill out to open your account. The new account form is the basic document the firm uses to supervise your account and to understand your objectives. From time to time, a broker will enter different information on the form than was given to him by the client. When filling out the new account form, some brokers may indicate more aggressive investment objectives than the client wants. Another section of the form that can be inflated by the broker is your income and net worth along with your past investing experience, which sets the stage for a possible defense in the event of a future problem.

Make sure you receive a filled-in copy of the new account form. Since this form is the basic document firms use to supervise your account, you want to know that it suits your investment needs. If the words *aggressive, short term, trading,* or *speculation* appear on the form, the supervisor overseeing your account will assume you want to be active and aggressive. Your account could be much more risky than you actually want. Do not open the account on your first visit to a broker.

Suitability

Your broker has the duty to recommend strategies and securities to you based on the information you give him. This is why the information on your new account form should be accurate and reflect your financial situation, experience and sophistication, and stated objectives. Investment objectives provided on the new account form are so important that I speak about them again separately, in Chapter 21.

NOTE

The new account form is the basic document the firm uses to supervise your account and to understand your objectives.

Suitability is an overarching principle of the brokerage industry. If you give your broker inaccurate information about yourself, he will act on that information. If the broker has distorted the information you gave him, you should contact the branch manager and probably find another broker possibly at another firm.

Income, Net Worth

A brokerage new account form asks for your income and net worth. A broker bases his suitability judgment on the financial data you provide along with your investment objective and experience. A brokerage firm defense against clients who seek redress of unsuitable activity, leading to losses, is that the client is wealthy and can afford the loss. Your financial data should be fairly stated, and the broker and the brokerage firm should be informed of your tolerance for risk and loss. However, you can't have it both ways. As already seen, you can't demand high growth and low risk.

CAUTION

Do not open the account on your first visit to a broker.

Investing Experience

Brokerage firms judge sophistication in investing based on your education, your investing history, and your exposure to market data from reading financial publications or watching stock market oriented television shows.

Supervision of Your Account

Whether you open an investment account with a brokerage firm, a bank, your accountant, an independent contractor (a broker who works independently but sends his trades to a firm organized to process trades of far-flung brokers), or your insurance agent who is licensed to sell stocks and mutual funds, you have to ask your potential broker and yourself who will supervise the broker looking after your financial welfare. Unless you open an account with a discount broker or an online broker, your brokerage account is a relationship with a firm and an individual who is going to recommend investments to you. If you select a broker who understands your investment objectives, however, and recommends only securities that are suitable for those objectives, you can have a long and successful relationship.

> **CAUTION**
> It is important to give your broker accurate information about yourself when you open your account.

Summary

Not everyone over 50 will want or need to open a brokerage account. Alternatives include investing directly with mutual fund companies, working with a money manager or trust officer of a bank. If you do open a brokerage account, pay close attention to the client agreement and the new account form, and remember that what you tell your broker will guide his activity. In the next few chapters, let's discuss how to direct the broker's activity and what to expect if something goes awry.

CHAPTER 21

Brokerage Account Investment Objectives and Happiness Letters

In earlier chapters, we talked about investment objectives in three broad terms: growth, income, and preservation of capital. As discussed in Chapter 20, when you open a brokerage account, your broker will fill out a new account form to open your account, and as part of that process, he will ask about your investment objectives.

Brokerage firms do not have a uniform set of investment objectives, but a look at the following general list of investment objectives will help you determine how to relate your objectives to your broker. These are the possible objectives you may come across on the new account form. They are all subtexts of the three objectives we have been discussing. They are organized here by increasing levels of risk:

- *Preservation of capital.* An objective of preservation of capital says you want no risk in your account. The account should have high-quality intermediate- to short-term bonds and money market funds or Treasury bills.

- *Income with low risk (bonds and preferred stocks).* If income with low risk is your objective, your account would invest in intermediate- and long-term bonds that have desirable investment characteristics. With this objective, your account would be subject to the fluctuations of the bond market but should avoid undue credit risk, compared with the following objective.

- *Income with high risk (high yield "junk bonds").* This investment objective is for the venturesome. The bonds in this account would be intermediate- to long-term bonds of lower quality and hence higher yield. The bonds could be subject to default and would expose you to considerable risk of loss. If higher yield is your objective and you are willing to assume the extra risk, it is often better to choose a well-managed high yield mutual fund than to have your broker sell you individual junk bonds.

- *Growth with income.* If you are in the 55-to-70 age bracket and have an investment portfolio you want to last through your life expectancy (if managed well), this is possibly the objective for you. This is a conservative objective. Your portfolio should consist of 40 percent to 60 percent bonds, with the balance in a diversified array of high-quality stocks. The bonds should provide you a good real rate of return (interest income minus inflation and taxes). If executed properly, you could expect the stock portfolio to approximate the return of the S&P 500 Index, discussed in Chapter 3.

- *Growth.* The experienced investor who is in the 50-to-60 age bracket can have a growth objective if the growth stocks are high quality, with solid franchises and a history of rising sales and earnings behind them. You would expect your account to track or slightly outperform the S&P 500 Index. A portfolio that performs at that level could double every 6 to 7 years and the beta (a form of volatility) would be slightly higher than the market. Such a portfolio should be diversified enough to eliminate single stock or industry risk and carry only market risk. Market risk is the risk inherent in the market in which you are investing. If the S&P 500 declines 10 percent, you would expect your portfolio to decline that much or slightly more.

NOTE
Review the investment objectives on your new account form with your broker for accuracy. What is on your new account form guides the broker. Those objectives will be held against you if there is a problem.

In a growth portfolio, your holding period should be measured in years rather than months.

- *Aggressive growth.* Aggressive growth would indicate that you want to invest in Internet, technology, and biotech stocks. The volatility of your portfolio would be much higher than a growth portfolio and your risk of loss would be much greater. Unless you have more wealth than you will need in your lifetime, this is not the objective for a soon-to-retire investor or a retired investor.

- *Trading.* An objective of trading says, "I want to play the market. I want to be in and out of stocks on a short-term basis. I know that my cost of trading could be a substantial portion of my investment. I want to take risk." Successful trading is usually done in a roaring bull market. Unfortunately, nobody rings a bell and says the party's over, sell now. Few investors trade successfully over the long term, including your broker. This objective is only suitable if you are wealthy beyond care.

- *Speculation.* An objective of speculation says, "I want to buy risky, unproven stocks in hopes of hitting tomorrow's Intel, Microsoft, or Cisco." You can plan on investing in 10 to 15 or more turkeys before you find the blue-bird of investment happiness you are seeking. Chances are that you are not going to stumble on tomorrow's great winner. Avoid this activity unless you have much more money than you will ever need.

> **NOTE**
>
> Brokerage firms systems alert branch managers to accounts they need to investigate. A lot of trading can be a red flag, as well as purchases that do not appear suited to the client's objectives.

It is important to review the investment objectives on your new account form with your broker for accuracy. Remember that what is on your new account form guides the broker. Those objectives will be held against you if there is a problem. One of the ways that a brokerage firm may contact you if it suspects a problem is with what is known in the industry as a *happiness letter.*

Happiness Letters

Brokerage firms have systems of supervision alerting branch managers to accounts they need to investigate. The red flags that cause an account to appear on the active account list are commissions in an amount that is a significant percentage of the account's net worth, churning, or unsuitable purchases. Churning is rapid turnover activity in an account for the purpose of generating commissions for the broker.

Most brokerage firms require that the manager write a letter (known in the business as a *happiness letter*) or call the client. A few brokerage firms have a policy of not articulating what they think the problem might be. The letter might merely say, "We appreciate your business and we hope you are happy with the transactions in your account and the service you receive. Please sign and return this letter to me to acknowledge that you have received and read it."

At times, brokers tell clients that a letter is coming from the manager, and to just sign it and send it back, or ignore it. Don't do this. If you receive such a letter, write the branch manager asking for a written response stating his concerns.

Summary

Your investment objectives will define how your account will be handled by your broker. Pay close attention to this part of the process to avoid unintended consequences. Be wary of brokers who befriend you and rely on your relationship to keep complaints from the manager. I often hear people say they don't want to get their brokers in trouble, even if they have been wronged. More often than not, other clients may have a similar problem with the broker. It is always best to be forthright; address questions and potential problems with the brokerage firm.

CHAPTER 22

Managing Your Brokerage Account

If you have a large sum of money to invest, you may decide to retain a money manager. If instead, you decide to work directly with a stockbroker, this chapter will help you understand what to expect on a day-to-day basis.

When your broker calls and recommends a transaction, he is working to close a sale. You need to ask questions, take notes, and ask the broker to mail printed material to you for your review. If you are at all uncertain about the product or the risk, tell him you don't understand why he is making the recommendation and ask him to explain that to you. If you can't turn around to a skeptical friend and explain what you are buying, why, and the risk you are assuming in exchange for the reward, turn it down. If you don't know what purpose it will serve in your overall portfolio, turn it down.

Getting Your Approval Prior to Making a Trade

A broker has no authority to transact in your account without your approval. Brokerage rules state that you can give your broker a limited power of attorney with the approval of his firm, also known as a discretionary account. Giving a broker such power demands that the brokerage firm give your account heightened supervision. Unauthorized trades are discussed in Chapter 24.

From time to time, a broker may feel free to make trades in customer accounts and then call the clients and inform them of the transactions. This is a violation of the rules governing broker behavior. If your broker makes an unauthorized trade in your account, call the broker and demand that the trade be canceled. Make a notation of the call in your calendar. If you do not receive a written confirmation of the cancellation in the mail within a few days, call the manager immediately and send him a letter or a fax demanding the trade be removed from your account. If you discuss this with the broker, he might say you will get him in trouble with the manager. He may even tell you he will take care of any losses should there be any. Losses are not the issue. Unauthorized activity is the problem. You do not want to give your broker the idea that you are willing to give him authority over the account. Say "no" to that proposal and immediately call and write the manager.

NOTE

A broker has no authority to transact in your account without your approval.

The broker who places unauthorized trades in your account is definitely not the broker you want. If you accept the trades, you have ratified his behavior and if losses ensue, you could have trouble getting the brokerage firm to make restitution. You could even be giving your broker de facto authorization to trade your account if you tolerate this behavior.

Reading Your Confirmations

There are two dates of importance on your confirmation, the *trade date* and the *settlement date*. The trade date is the date the trade is executed, and the settlement date is the date money and securities must change hands to complete the trade. If you have not delivered your securities or payment to the brokerage firm by settlement date, the firm will start notifying you of your delinquency and prepare to buy in your sale or sell out your purchase and charge any loss to your account. Brokerage firms are governed by rules that give them little discretion in handling these matters.

A confirmation reports the details of a single transaction at a time. Your confirmation will tell you that you sold (or bought) 500 shares of

XYZ Company at $50.00 per share for a gross amount of $25,000. You will also see commissions and fees reflected in the gross amount. (If you bought, commissions and fees are added to the gross amount. If you sold, they are deducted.) Fees can be nominal SEC fees, and postage and handling of $2.50 or more. Some postage and handling fees go as high as $7.50.

Commissions are charged for transactions in which the broker acted as your agent and sold or bought your securities in a transaction with third parties, usually through an execution on an exchange.

The broker can also act as principal instead of agent. In that case, he is buying or selling securities from the brokerage firm's account. If the broker acted as principal, instead of a commission, you will see a markup (or markdown) added to the market price of the security. In the case of bonds, you will not see any reference to markups (or markdowns) on the confirmation. You will only see the bond, the number of bonds in the transaction, the price per bond, and the gross amount. Your confirmation will also show accrued interest on the bonds.

> **NOTE**
>
> Commissions are charged for transactions in which the broker acted as your agent and sold or bought your securities in a transaction with third parties, usually through an execution on an exchange.

Stock transactions are required by SEC rule 10b-10 to show the markup (or markdown), but only if it is above or below the National Best Bid and Offer. The National Best Bid and Offer is the best bid at which a stock can be sold and the best offer at which the stock can be bought. Let's say the stock you bought was 20.50 bid, 21.00 offered, and your broker charged you 25 cents per share for your transaction. Since the markup is above the price at which the stock can be bought, your confirmation will show the firm sold to you 500 shares of XYZ Corporation at 21.25, with a markup of 25 cents. The confirmation will also state: "Our firm makes a market in this security." This means that the firm buys and sells the security in question for its own trading account. The broker may also receive an extra payment called a "sales credit" from the department that trades the security as part of the spread between 20.50 and 21.00.

Check the confirmation to determine that this is the transaction you ordered. If your confirmation says "as of xx/xx/xx" date, your trade was not entered into the firm's operations system on the date of the transaction, and you should ask the broker what caused it to be entered late.

You should read the fine print on the front and back of the confirmation slip. It tells you where the trade was executed, the role of the broker (principal or agent), and informs you that if you think there is an error on the trade you have five days to report it to the firm in writing. That reporting is a duty the brokerage firm has assigned to you. It is part of state commercial laws.

Reading Your Monthly Statement

Your monthly statement contains all the trading that settled within the month. It includes interest and dividends received and deposits and withdrawals. The statement has a listing of your month-end portfolio and its value plus any cash balances or money market balances in your account. It is hard to tell if you have a margin account on some statements, but if you see that you have been charged interest or if your cash balance is a negative number, you have a margin account. If you have a cash account, you will not see negative cash balances or interest charges. If you find an error in your account, report it immediately to your broker in writing. Margin accounts are covered in Chapter 23.

Importantly, compare the preceding month's value of your account with this month's value and compare this month's value to your December 31 statement of the past year. This helps you determine your performance. Of course, you will have to adjust all comparison numbers for deposits and withdrawals. Some people keep a handwritten ledger of all moneys they have added to the account throughout the year and all the money they have withdrawn. Then, they compare their performance, adjusted for those cash flows.

Trade Errors

From time to time, a broker will make an error in entering an order in an account. The error could be that he entered a "buy" order instead of a "sell" order, he entered a wrong account number on the order ticket, or he bought or sold the wrong stock. If you did not give the erroneous instructions to him, your broker is responsible for the error. Make sure you bring the error to his attention, and it should be corrected in your account in one or two days. If it is not corrected, call the branch manager and send a letter or a fax to confirm that you understand he will correct it.

Discount and Online Brokerage Accounts

In return for lower commissions offered by discount and online firms, you act as your own adviser. You take responsibility for trade errors. The brokerage firm is still responsible for its own errors, but you have a heightened duty to read your confirmations and monthly statements. This is simply because you do not have a broker and his assistant checking the order tickets against confirmations. You are also responsible for the suitability of the investments you select on your own.

Another burden you assume when you open an online brokerage account is that you need to be familiar with industry rules and practices. You have to know how to place an order to buy or sell and you have to know the ramifications of placing each kind of order. If you place a market order, it is executed at the prevailing price at the time the order reaches the place of execution, be it the Nasdaq market or the floor of the New York Stock Exchange. A volatile stock or an initial public offering that has just come to market might be 10, 20, or more points away from the price it traded at when you decided to enter an order.

> **CAUTION**
>
> Another burden you assume when you open an online brokerage account is that you need to be familiar with industry rules and practices.

Many older investors were badly burned chasing initial public offerings (IPOs) through online trading in the Internet bubble of 1999–2000. Unwary investors who placed market orders bought on the top of the initial market spike only to see the price fall 30 percent or more, wiping out their accounts. There are cases of elderly investors with margin accounts who placed market orders for 10,000 shares of an IPO assuming they would get the stock at around a $15 initial price. Instead, the orders were filled at $50 or more per share getting them a huge margin call and a financially crippling loss.

Types of orders you need to be familiar with are market orders, which execute immediately at best available price; limit orders, which execute at the stated price or better today only; good-the-week (GTW) limit orders, which execute at this price or better this week ending this Friday. There are also good-the-month and good-until-canceled orders. Stop orders are triggered when a stock rises or falls to the stated price. Stop orders can be market or limit orders. (Keep in mind that the market stop order can execute above or below the specified price.) A stop limit order can only be executed at the stated price, and it will be unexecuted if the market moves through and beyond the price limit.

Another type of order is the all-or-none order. It is just as it says, "Execute this order for the full amount at this price or do none of it." Investors enter a large all-or-none order and question why there was no execution of their order even though there was good trading volume during the day at or above their limit price. The answer is that there was not a buyer or seller willing to transact just that size at just that price. Your online broker should have material explaining these orders to you and how to place them. Some may limit the types of orders they will accept.

Summary

How you approach your brokerage account will depend somewhat on whether you do it yourself online or with a stockbroker affiliated with a brokerage firm. You are the first line of defense in either case. You must give close attention to every confirmation and monthly statement you receive. In return for the discount you receive with an online account, you assume a higher level of care and must educate yourself about stocks and brokerage practices to manage and monitor your account.

CHAPTER 23

Margin

Brokerage firms will lend you money to buy securities, provided you give them collateral to secure the loan. This means that investors have to pledge the securities in their brokerage accounts to receive the loans, which are called *margin loans* or simply, *margin*. Since the margin agreement may be contained in the agreement that you signed when you opened your account, you may have pledged the securities in your account without knowing it. Check to see whether you have a *margin account* or a *cash account*. The former involves the extension of credit and the latter does not.

Using margin leverages your money. That is, you need less to buy more. That could be good if the stocks you buy go up in value. Or it could be bad if the stocks you buy go down in value. Compare margin with a mortgage to buy a house. Most people do not have enough money to pay for a house in full. They borrow money from a bank, which the bank secures with the home as collateral. Similarly, a brokerage firm will lend you money to buy stocks, securing your obligation to repay the loan with the stocks in your account.

If you continue making payments on the mortgage as agreed, the bank will not sell your home out from under you. Similarly, the brokerage firm will not sell your stocks if you keep up your obligation to maintain sufficient *credit balances* or *equity* in your brokerage account to secure the debt you owe the brokerage firm. However, we are not talking about making monthly margin payments as you would monthly mortgage payments. Since the stocks you bought with borrowed money fluctuate in value every day, the brokerage firm values your account every day to see if your collateral is sufficient to support the loan. If it falls below certain levels, which I discuss later in this chapter, the firm will sell your stocks, like it or not. This is the crux of the problem that people face with a margin loan, getting sold out at the bottom of the market.

CAUTION

Since the margin agreement may be contained in the agreement that you signed when you opened your account, you may have pledged the securities in your account without knowing it.

Read your margin agreement. The language is stern. The firm is under no obligation to call you prior to selling out your account. In fact, the brokerage firm has the duty to protect itself and its other customers from credit losses that result from under-margined accounts. The brokerage firm's ability to maintain its own capital is carefully scrutinized by the regulators. The Federal Reserve Bank does not want the brokerage firm to extend credit beyond its means, which would jeopardize the firm's own capital and the accounts of other customers.

Regulation

When you agree to open a margin account, you are giving up a certain amount of control. In effect, control goes to the brokerage firm that is extending you credit to buy or carry investments in your account. The brokerage firm itself is under a legal duty to take action against accounts that fall below certain levels.

The federal law that regulates the extension of credit for securities purchases is Regulation T ("Reg T"), under the supervision of the Federal Reserve Bank. Regulation T says that the broker cannot extend more than 50 percent credit to you in making a purchase and that you will pay for your stocks (cash or margin accounts) within a certain time. Under Reg T, on the fifth day after your trade (settlement plus two), you must have paid for the transaction or the brokerage firm has to sell out your position or ask the New York Stock Exchange for an extension of time for a valid reason. One valid reason is "the check is in the mail." If your purchase is liquidated, you are responsible for any loss and your account is restricted for 90 days to trades covered by cash in your account.

If you are *on margin,* you have borrowed money from the brokerage firm to carry your stocks. You must maintain your *equity* at certain levels. Your equity is the value of the marginable securities in your account minus the debt you owe the brokerage firm. Typically, you will need to deposit 50 percent of the purchase price of the security you want to buy, and the brokerage firm will lend you the remaining 50 percent at the firm's "margin rate." The firm's margin rate is typically a premium of up to two percentage points above the "broker call rate," which is set by prevailing market rates and published in the *Wall Street Journal.* You are obligated to pay interest to the brokerage firm at the firm's margin rate on the amount you borrowed until the loan is repaid. Your margin balance creates a "debit," which is your obligation to the brokerage firm.

There are three kinds of margin calls: A "Reg T" call, which is on your initial purchase; a "maintenance" call, which usually means that if your equity is below 35 percent the brokerage firm will call you asking you to bring your equity back up to the 35 percent level; and a "Stock Exchange" call, which means your equity is below 25 percent of the value of your account and the Exchange requires the brokerage firm to have you deposit funds to bring your equity back to more than 25 percent or sell enough from your account to raise your equity. If the brokerage firm does not accomplish this in a short time, the Exchange requires the firm to charge its capital with the deficiency. Brokerage firms are understandably reluctant to take a charge to their capital for your benefit, so they sell you out.

CAUTION

Read your margin agreement. The language is stern. The firm is under no obligation to call you prior to selling out your account.

When you margin your brokerage account, you add a speculative element to your investing. If you borrow 50 percent on your stocks and your portfolio declines by 25 percent, a number certainly not unheard of even in moderate markets, you will have to satisfy a maintenance call. You must send in a check or some securities in your account will be sold. If you suffer a decline of 35 percent, you will receive a Stock Exchange call and face a sellout.

For example, assume your portfolio is worth $10,000. Because you borrowed $5,000 from the brokerage firm to buy the stock, your equity is $5,000. The stock drops by 25 percent to $7,500. What is your equity now? $2,500. ($7,500 less $5,000, which is the amount you owe the brokerage firm.) You will receive a maintenance call because your equity is now below the 35 percent maintenance level referred to above. ($2,500 divided by $7,500 is 33.3 percent.)

Margining your account can make it impossible for you to survive even a moderate sell-off in the market. While margin can allow you to participate two for one on the upside, the dangers on the downside are enough to make the investor who is at or near retirement want to avoid the risk.

Margin as an Indicator

One of the market indicators that we watch is customer margin borrowing, which is available through the Federal Reserve. The higher the extension of credit, the bigger the potential downside risk can be in the market overall. We have seen a great deal of growth in borrowing over the past few years. In October 2000, for example, debit balances at New York Stock Exchange registered brokerage firms represented $233 billion.

NOTE

When you margin your brokerage account, you add a speculative element to your investing.

Compare three years earlier. For the month of October 1997, there was $128 billion outstanding in debit balances, about one half of the October 2000 experience.

Summary

Experienced stock market investors know that when the market is in a downtrend, the final down thrust is the day that the margin accounts that were not brought up to acceptable levels are liquidated. The added reward of doubling your participation on the upside brings a greater risk of significant loss when the market swings to the downside. Avoid that added risk if you are in or approaching retirement.

CHAPTER 24

What the Industry Regulations Say about Your Brokerage Account

In this chapter, I discuss industry rules governing broker-client relations. We touched on a few of these issues in Chapter 20. This chapter gives you more detail and more information about what to do if you sense you might need help with a problem. This discussion includes churning, unsuitability of risky investments and options, unauthorized trades, and selling away. At the end of the chapter, I discuss in a little more detail how to bring a problem to the attention of the brokerage firm for resolution, and if you cannot achieve resolution, other avenues you can pursue, including arbitration.

Churning Stocks

Churning is a pattern of trading that a broker undertakes to generate commissions for himself. Although churning can be hard to detect on a day-to-day basis or from reviewing a monthly statement, you can apply some measures to see if there is excessive trading in your account. If your account has turned over more than twice a year, you may have been churned. For example, your account has stocks with a value of $100,000. If your broker sells those stocks and buys

$100,000 worth of different stocks, your account has been turned over once. If he does that again within a year, you have a turnover rate of two times, which can be an inference of churning. Turnover of six times is considered churning under most circumstances. Some churned accounts have a turnover rate of 10 to 30 times or more. Remember that each buy or sell transaction results in a commission.

Another measure of churning is based on commissions as a percentage of your account value. Known as *cost/equity ratio*, it is the total of all the commissions charged to your account divided by your account's value (equity). If your cost/equity is 6 percent or above, the account should be examined for churning. In egregious cases, the cost/equity ratio can be as high as 30 percent to 40 percent. That would mean that if your account is worth $100,000, you are paying commissions of $30,000 to $40,000 a year. If your account is very active, add up the commissions listed on your confirmations and compare that number to your equity and to the profit in your account.

In Chapter 21, we discussed happiness letters. Most of the time, happiness letters are generated because of high turnover or commissions. If you get such a letter, call the branch manager and ask him what concerns him about your account. Take notes of the answers you are given. If there is excessive activity or commissions in your account, ask how he is going to resolve the problem. Do not sign and return the happiness letter under any circumstances. If you suspect untoward activity, you may wish to involve a lawyer before you put anything in writing.

Churning or Switching Mutual Funds

While a mutual fund is designed as a long-term investment, mutual funds can also be churned and "switched." A greedy broker can take advantage of unsuspecting clients by moving the client from one fund family that charges a commission to another. A family is a set of funds offered by a single sponsor and provides an array of funds to meet different investment objectives. Movement within a family of funds is typically free of commissions and costs. If the fund you own needs to be replaced, there should be a suitable fund in the family to which it belongs, and there should be no cost to make a change. If your broker feels strongly that you should switch to another family, he should be able to satisfy you and the branch manager as to why you had to leave one fund family and pay a commission to buy a fund in a different family. Also, commission rates (or loads) decrease at different "breakpoints": The more you invest in a single fund family, the lower the commission rate, going to zero above $1 million. Beware of brokers splitting your investment among a number of fund families to earn a higher commission.

> **CAUTION**
>
> Beware of brokers splitting your investment among a number of fund families to earn a higher commission.

Churning Bonds

Bonds are another product where a broker can do some creative churning. Bonds trade in an over-the-counter market. Over-the-counter means that trades are not executed through an exchange, such as the New York Stock Exchange. Your broker will usually sell you bonds from the firm's inventory. Many times a broker sells you a bond with a longer maturity or a lower quality rating to show you a higher return to entice you to make the trade. Brokers who churn bonds will sell you a bond with a hefty markup, then as the price rises to allow you to sell the bond at the price you paid, the broker will suggest selling your bond and buying another. You don't lose any money, but you have a much lower return on your investments than you deserve.

While the number of trades in bond churning will not be as frequently as in stock churning, the broker is well compensated when you *trade* your bonds. The bonds he trades have a markup and possibly an additional special sales credit for the broker that he can get when you sell a bond, followed by another sales credit when you buy the replacement bond. The total sales compensation to a broker on a purchase of a single bond can range from 1 percent to 4 or 5 percent of your investment.

> **NOTE**
>
> The total sales compensation to a broker on a purchase of a single bond can range from 1 percent to 4 or 5 percent of your investment.

Unsuitability

Risky stocks may not be appropriate investments for conservative investors over 50. The same is true of risky corporate bonds, municipal bonds, mutual funds, and options. A broker is required to know the investment and risk characteristics of the securities he recommends. He is required under industry rules to recommend only those securities that are suitable for your investment objective and risk profile. For example, a biotech company with untested products in its pipeline would not be a suitable investment for a conservative investor. On the other hand, such a company could be suitable for an investor with an aggressive growth objective. Look at your account and ask yourself if you know the investment characteristics of your holdings. If not, a trip to your library and some time spent with the Value Line Investment Survey or Standard & Poor's Outlook or similar publications should help you determine if your holdings match your investment needs. Brokerage accounts seldom migrate to the overly conservative since many brokers, particularly younger ones, tend to be aggressive and look for stocks that will appreciate in a relatively short period so they can take profits and earn a commission. Be aware.

NOTE

A broker is required to know the investment and risk characteristics of the securities he recommends. He is required under industry rules to recommend only those securities that are suitable for your investment objective and risk profile.

Options

Option strategies are often suggested by a broker to "enhance your income." While we won't go into those strategies here, be aware that options are high-income generators for the broker as a percentage of the amount invested. Since options expire, they have a short life for the client; your agreement to enter into an options trading program can pay the broker handsomely.

Also, be aware that by writing an option against a position you own (giving someone the right to call the stock away from you at a stated price), you give up profit potential. If you buy a call or a put option, you are betting on price movement. Options are best left to younger, more aggressive investors who have time to make up losses through other investments or earnings. Be careful if your broker suggests options and be particularly careful about the information and objectives entered on the options suitability form. Never sign a blank options form.

CAUTION

Be careful if your broker suggests options and be particularly careful about the information and objectives entered on the options suitability form. Never sign a blank options form.

Unauthorized Transactions

We spoke about unauthorized transactions briefly in Chapter 20. If you notice a trade on a confirmation or account statement that you did not authorize, immediately call the branch manager. If the trade was an honest mistake, the manager will be sure it is corrected. If the trade was an unauthorized transaction, the manager will have to have a session with the broker. In either case, the broker will be alerted that you are watching your account and that you will tolerate no deviation from the rules. An unscrupulous broker will test clients to see if they complain about unauthorized trades and will continue to make them and "sell" the customer on accepting them after he has made them. The end result can be disastrous for the customer who allows it.

Selling Away

Your broker may sell you investments through the brokerage firm he works for, but not outside investments. *Selling away* occurs when your broker offers you a "private investment" that his firm is not offering. The investment could be a participation in a new company, an interest-bearing note, or other fixed income instrument from a private investor. Brokers have also offered "prime bank" loans, some of which are known to be scams. Every now and then brokers engage in *Ponzi schemes* in which they borrow money

> ◣ **CAUTION**
>
> **An unscrupulous broker will test clients to see if they complain about unauthorized trades and will continue to make them and "sell" the customer on accepting them after he has made them.**

from clients and use new money they have borrowed to pay the interest obligations to existing holders. A Ponzi scheme is a phony investment in which a current investor is paid from money new investors put into the scheme.

Never have a private transaction with your broker in which you give or lend him money. Brokerage firms monitor accounts, so brokers who want to obtain money from clients will usually send the client a check from the client's account and ask the client to send back a personal check. That way, the brokerage firm cannot detect the fraud or infraction of their rules.

Resolving Problems with the Brokerage Firm

When you detect a problem with your account, or do not understand the activity in your account, ask your broker for an explanation. If there is no resolution, call the branch manager. The manager will probably be able to take care of the problem within a couple of days if the problem is an error or wrong trade in your account. If you are claiming that a trade or series of trades was unauthorized or unsuitable, the manager will have to investigate the facts and get back to you. If the problem is not resolved, or the manager tells you that your claim has no merit, you may have to write the firm's legal or compliance department about your problem. These departments will be located at the firm's headquarters, which is listed on your monthly statement. If the legal or compliance department does not give you a reasonable answer, you may have to seek outside help in resolving your problem. Lawyers who specialize in investor disputes with stockbrokers will want you to contact them first before calling or writing to the branch manager or compliance departments.

Every state has a securities department that regulates brokerage activity in that state. You can find the address by contacting either the Attorney General's office or the Department of Consumer Affairs. If neither of these departments handles securities matters, you will be referred to the department that does. Have your facts and collect all documents that relate to the problem. If you do not get a satisfactory resolution, you can take your problem to any one of the following: the National Association of Securities Dealers, The New York Stock Exchange, or the Securities and Exchange Commission. Do not take it to more than one regulator because a problem becomes important to no one if too many entities are trying to solve it.

> **NOTE**
>
> A Ponzi scheme is a phony investment in which a current investor is paid from money new investors put into the scheme.

If your problem involves a considerable loss of money, you might want to contact your attorney or an attorney who has securities experience. Often, an experienced attorney can resolve the problem with the brokerage firm without having to file an arbitration claim.

Your lawyer will usually try to settle the matter prior to arbitration either by direct negotiation or mediation. If the case is not settled, it will be heard by a panel of three arbitrators, two of whom are from the "public." The third is an "industry" arbitrator. A public arbitrator is not employed by the brokerage industry, while the industry arbitrator is usually employed by a brokerage firm. The cost of the arbitration, which includes arbitrator fees and the use of the arbitration facilities of the self-regulatory organization providing the arbitration forum, will be allocated by the panel.

Statistics about the chances of an award in arbitration have been studied and published by the General Accounting Office in Washington. This report is available online or through the Government Printing Office. In reading those statistics, keep in mind that the data covers cases brought to hearing after there was no resolution in negotiation or mediation, so you are looking at the resolution of the most difficult or contentious problems. Your attorney can advise you of the merits of your case and your chances of prevailing.

> **TIP**
>
> If the legal or compliance department does not give you a reasonable answer, you may have to seek outside help in resolving your problem.

Summary

It is helpful to know about some of the standards that apply to brokerage account activity so that you can recognize churning, switching, unsuitable trading, unauthorized trading, and selling away. In the event you are confused by the activity in the account, it is always best to seek an explanation that is satisfactory to you. If you suspect untoward activity, take it seriously.

CHAPTER 25

Tax Considerations

In this chapter, I have asked tax expert, Manny Bernardo, JD, formerly head of the Deloitte & Touche, LLP, Connecticut Compensation and Benefits Tax Practice, to give you an overview of the tax laws that affect investments. These begin on page 147. First, a caution: Many times, investors want to avoid taxes at all costs. If you are successful at investing, you will take profits and receive distributions, which are going to be taxable. You can refrain from selling stocks at a profit to avoid a taxable event, thus saving you tax dollars, but that strategy can also prevent you from ever making any money. The idea behind investing is to make money, and in most cases that means sharing it with the government sooner or later.

This chapter deals with taxable investment activity. Tax-deferred investing through your company sponsored saving plan or Individual Retirement Account (IRA) is covered in Chapter 26, and because they are taxed differently, Roth IRAs are covered in Chapter 27. This chapter is intended as a bare-bones minimum tax review. The Internal Revenue Service (IRS) provides many useful tax publications about the taxation of investments and can offer more complete information than can be included here. Some of the publications are mentioned in the following text. All are available for free by calling 1-800-TAX-FORM. In addition, you will need to review your tax situation with your tax adviser before making any tax decisions.

People who look for investments that avoid taxes can find themselves paying more in the long run. Take the popular tax shelters sold by brokerage firms in the 1980s. Tax shelters were attractive because they accelerated tax deductions or credits, and permitted taxpayers to reduce the taxes they paid on *other* income. Acceleration involved gathering future tax deductions or credits into the present. Many of these taxes shelters came back to haunt investors. Many are still paying taxes on *phantom* income, which is income they do not receive, but is nonetheless taxable since it must be reported by the tax shelter.

NOTE

The idea behind investing is to make money, and in most cases that means sharing it with the government sooner or later.

This does not mean that investors should ignore taxes and tax consequences when making investment decisions—only that tax considerations should not dictate investment decisions. As one accountant put it, "The tail should not wag the dog." Tax considerations are often considered, however, together with investment objectives and risk tolerance and other factors, in selecting investments for a portfolio. In addition, tax considerations can be a factor in deciding when to buy or sell investments.

A couple of examples may be helpful. Long-term capital gain rates are generally lower than ordinary income tax rates that apply to short-term gains (generally 20% vs. 28% or higher). Therefore, if other investment considerations, such as risk, do not dictate otherwise, it sometimes makes sense to hold an investment until after a full year of ownership has passed, in order to pay the lower tax rate. You may also have a reason to sell a holding at a loss for a tax deduction, while replacing it with a similar investment. Rules against "wash sales" preclude a tax deduction if you repurchase the same security within a 30-day period.

Taxes Applicable to Investments

The United States Internal Revenue Code defines income for federal tax purposes as "all income from whatever source derived" (Code Section 61(a)). The same Code section enumerates specific types of income that are generated by investments—including gains from dealing in property, interest, and dividends. All income is subject to federal tax, unless expressly excluded or specifically made subject to particular tax rules, for example, capital gains. Although many states' tax laws mirror the federal tax law, you should always consult your own tax adviser regarding federal and state tax consequences of a transaction or investment.

Overview of Federal Tax Rules

Interest Income

All bond interest is fully taxable, except for tax-exempt state or municipal bonds. Most individuals are "cash basis" taxpayers, which means that interest is taxable in the year in which it is received. However, interest on bank deposits, interest payable on bond coupons, and similar interest payments are deemed to be available when credited or payable, even if the individual taxpayer does not withdraw the bank interest or cash in the bond coupon. Therefore, you are subject to income tax on bank savings account interest credited to your account during a tax year, even if you do not withdraw the interest. The same is true for interest you can receive for cashing in bond coupons payable on December 15, even if you delay cashing in such coupons until after the end of the year.

> **CAUTION**
>
> This does not mean that investors should ignore taxes and tax consequences when making investment decisions—only that tax considerations should not dictate investment decisions.

Imputed Interest

Often bonds or other debt obligations are issued and sold at a discount equaling the interest that would have been earned over the life of the obligation. Common examples are "zero coupon" bonds (discussed in Chapter 16) or certificates that grow in value each year by an amount equal to the deemed interest discount. Sometimes the discounts are called *Original Issue Discounts* (OIDs). The amount of increase in value each year is taxable as interest income in such year. If no specific amount of annual increase in value is stated, the total increase in value over the life of the bond must be amortized and recognized as taxable interest each year.

For example, a company can issue either a typical $500 bond at 9 percent interest, or a discounted $1,000 8-year bond for which it receives $500 on issue, which is a discount of $500 from $1,000. With the typical bond, the company pays out interest during the year, and you pay taxes on the interest you receive every year. Then, the company redeems the bond at maturity for $500, which is the amount of your original investment.

With a zero coupon bond, which is a discount bond, the company pays no interest during the year; instead you get the interest in a single lump sum when you redeem the bond at maturity. That is, you would receive $1,000 at maturity, with $500 representing your original investment and the other $500 representing your interest. But, that does not mean you can wait until maturity to pay taxes on the $500 interest the bond is accreting. Each year, you need to amortize the interest, so that it is recognized as taxable income each taxable year during your holding period. Whether you buy the typical bond paying interest during the holding period or the discounted bond, which pays the interest at redemption, you would recognize roughly the same amount of taxable interest income each year.

Dividends

NOTE

Some mutual fund distributions are subject to different tax treatment.

Generally, dividends are fully taxable in the tax year in which they are declared and payable or credited to the taxpayer's account, whether or not they are withdrawn. Dividends include typical dividends paid by corporations on their stock, as well as dividend distributions by regulated investment companies, generally known as mutual funds, whether paid out in cash or credited to shareholders' accounts and reinvested. Dividend distributions by mutual funds that invest in municipal bonds are considered dividends, but are tax-exempt to the same extent the interest received by the mutual fund would be tax-exempt interest.

Some mutual fund distributions are subject to different tax treatment. Gains realized by mutual funds on the sale of securities within their portfolios are distributed as capital gains distributions, and are treated as capital gains (not dividends). The funds' long-term capital gains are taxable as long-term capital gains in the tax year in which the fund sold the securities. The Form 1099 that you receive from the fund after the end of the year indicates how much you received from the fund in taxable capital gains distributions, both long and short, as well as dividends for the year, so that you can report them on your tax return.

Gains from Dealing in Property

Gains from the sale or exchange of property, including stocks and bonds and mutual fund shares, must be recognized for income tax purposes. Usually, the gain that must be recognized equals the amount received, reduced by the *adjusted basis* of the property. Adjusted basis equals the original cost of the property plus costs of acquiring and selling the property, such as brokerage commissions. Sales commissions on mutual funds count toward the adjusted basis, thus decreasing your taxable gain. For example, if you buy a mutual fund $10 per share and the sales commission or load is $1, your adjusted basis is $11. If you sell for $12, your taxable gain will be only $1 not $2. If you sold after holding on to the share for more than 12 months, your tax is 20 percent of $1 or 20 cents per share. If you sold after less than 12 months, your tax is determined at ordinary income tax rates that apply to your personal situation. You can look up your rate in the tax tables provided in the instructions to IRS Form 1040. If an investment has generated depreciation or depletion deductions, the adjusted basis is reduced by the full amount of such deductions.

Short-term capital gains are taxed at ordinary income rates, just like interest and dividends. Long-term capital gains are generally taxed at the lower of the taxpayer's ordinary income tax rate or the long-term capital gains rate of 20 percent. A capital gain is long-term if the asset has been held over one year. A lower long-term capital gains rate of 18 percent (8% for 15% bracket taxpayers) will apply to capital assets acquired after December 31, 2000, and held for at least five years.

NOTE

A capital gain is long-term if the asset has been held over one year.

For example, if John Doe, a 28 percent bracket taxpayer, buys 100 shares of X stock at $10 per share plus 50 cents per share commission, and sells the stock for $15 per share less 50 cents per share commission, he will have a capital gain of $4 per share ($15 received less $10 cost plus $1 commissions). If he had held the stock more than one year, he would pay tax on the $4 per share at a 20 percent rate. If he owned the stock less than one year, he would pay a 28 percent tax on the $4.

If John Doe were a 15 percent bracket taxpayer, he would pay 15 percent tax on the $4 per share, because his ordinary income tax rate is lower than the maximum long-term capital gains tax rate. To be in the 15 percent bracket, John's taxable income would have to be less than $26,250 if he were single and less than $43,850 if he were married filing jointly (under year 2000 tax tables).

Capital Losses

Capital losses occur when the adjusted basis of property exceeds the amount received on the sale of the property. Short-term capital losses must first be applied to reduce short-term capital gains, and long-term capital losses must first be applied to reduce long-term capital gains. Excess short-term capital losses then reduce long-term capital gains, if any, and excess long-term capital losses reduce short-term capital gains. If capital losses exceed all capital gains, then such losses (up to $3,000) may be deducted, that is, used to reduce taxable ordinary income. If any capital loss remains, it may be carried over and applied to reduce future capital gains or ordinary income.

Tax-Exempt Investments

Obligations of a state, territory, or possession of the United States, or of any political subdivision of any of the foregoing, or of the District of Columbia, generally called municipal bonds, are tax-exempt instruments. This means that interest payable with respect to all such obligations is not subject to federal income tax. Generally, interest on tax-exempt instruments of a state or a political subdivision of a state is exempt from income taxes for that state, but usually is subject to state income taxes of other states.

NOTE

Tax-exempt instruments are not exempt from capital gains taxes and the mutual fund capital gains distribution tax rules.

Obligations issued by the federal government are exempt from all state and local income taxes, but are subject to federal income taxes. Dividends paid or credited by mutual funds that invest in tax-exempt instruments or federal obligations are subject to the preceding tax rules, just like interest paid directly on tax-exempt obligations. Tax-exempt instruments are not exempt from capital gains taxes and the mutual fund capital gains distribution tax rules reviewed earlier.

Summary

In light of the foregoing, tax-exempt instruments may have a role in your investment portfolio, although, as discussed, tax considerations should not be the primary determinant of any investment decision. For example, if tax-exempt instruments (which are not included in calculating adjusted gross income for federal taxes) yield approximately the same after-tax return as taxable instruments (which are included in adjusted gross income), including some tax-exempt securities or mutual funds in your portfolio may help preserve tax deductions and exemptions that might otherwise be partially phased out if your adjusted gross income were higher. You should consult your tax adviser for specific advice.

CHAPTER 26

Tax-Deferred Company Savings Plans, IRAs, and Variable Annuities

You have some choices as to how to invest for retirement. When you put money into your savings account or buy stocks through your brokerage account, your investment activity results in income and gains that will be taxed yearly, as discussed in Chapter 25. Or, you can defer current taxes until after retirement, which is the subject of this chapter. If you qualify, your investment can grow essentially tax-free through a Roth IRA, discussed in Chapter 27.

There are at least three ways you can invest for retirement on a tax-deferred basis: a company savings plan, a traditional Individual Retirement Account (IRA), and a tax-deferred variable annuity. Depending on your particular circumstances, you may find that you need to invest in more than one type of tax-deferred account to maximize your retirement benefits.

Tax-Deferred Company Plans

There are a number of different types of company savings plans for which you may be eligible. If you work at a for-profit company, you may have a 401(k) plan. While the law permits 401(k) plans for nonprofits, most offer tax-sheltered annuities or 403(b) plans, which are similar in concept to 401(k) plans from a tax point of view and may offer employer contributions. State and local government plans and some nonprofit plans are called 457 plans. All these plans have similarities. Here, we'll focus on the most popular, the 401(k) plan.

A 401(k) plan is a company savings plan to which employees contribute through regular payroll deductions. Depending on the plan, the company may also contribute to your account, sometimes in proportion to your contribution.

One of the compelling benefits of the 401(k) as a savings vehicle is the pretax nature of the employee contributions and the tax deferral on company contributions, translating into meaningful tax savings for the participant. What it actually costs an individual to contribute to his plan can be a fraction of the dollar amount that flows into the account on the participant's behalf.

Grace, a person who earns $30,000 a year, or about $580 a week, illustrates this point. Grace signs up for a 6 percent pretax contribution to her plan. At 6 percent, she contributes $1,800 into the plan that year. However, her payroll department withholds taxes for her as if she were making $28,200 instead of $30,000 ($30,000 minus $1,800).

NOTE

There are two types of IRAs: a "traditional IRA" and a "Roth IRA." A traditional IRA is tax-deferred. A Roth investment can grow essentially tax free.

Grace's 401(k) plan has a 50 percent match. That means her company matches her contribution 50 cents on the dollar. For every dollar Grace puts in, her company adds 50 cents on her behalf. Because Grace is putting $1,800 into her plan, her company's 50 percent match amounts to $900. Adding those two numbers shows that $2,700 is going into Grace's 401(k) account that year. In this example, Grace's match vests immediately, which means that she doesn't have to fulfill a waiting period before it is hers to take out of the plan should she leave or retire.

Because of the match, Grace's company is paying her more than her salary of $30,000. Due to the match of $900, she is actually earning $30,900 that year. A match is a *bonus* you get from the company only if you qualify by participating in the plan. Matches range from zero to 50 percent, 100 percent, or even 200 percent, depending on your company's plan.

Tax Benefits

At tax time, you would expect that Grace's W-2 would show taxable earnings that included not only Grace's salary of $30,000 but also the full amount of the company's match of $900, bringing the total W-2 earnings to $30,900. But, this does not happen. Grace's W-2 does *not* include the money she contributes to her 401(k). Moreover, it does not include the matching money her company pays into her account. And, it does not include any money she earns on her 401(k) investments. To recap, instead of showing $30,900 ($30,000 plus her $900 match), Grace's W-2 shows only $28,200 ($30,000 earnings minus her pretax contribution of $1,800).

Cost to Participant

It is also helpful to figure how much the participant is actually paying into the 401(k) and compare what he is getting in return. The cost to Grace is her 6 percent contribution for the year, which totals $1,800. This needs to be offset by the $270 she saves in taxes because of her participation (this assumes Grace is in the 15 percent tax bracket). That's $1,800 minus $270 in tax savings, which equals $1,530. So, Grace pays $1,530 for her 401(k) account.

Compare what she receives in return. First, count the $1,800 she puts into her account through payroll deductions. Then, add the $900 match her company puts up. That brings us to $2,700. To be fair, you would also add her growth and earnings on her 401(k) investments, but because that varies from year to year, we won't do that here.

> **NOTE**
>
> A match is a bonus you get from the company only if you qualify by participating in the plan. Matches range from zero to 50 percent, 100 percent, or even 200 percent, depending on your company's plan.

Now, let's see if Grace gets what she pays for. Grace gets $2,700 worth of 401(k) benefits, plus earnings on her investments, while paying only $1,530. That's a return of $1,170 on an investment of $1,530 in one year. You could not make that kind of return outside your 401(k) account without taking on a very high level of risk.

Benefits of Participating in Your 401(k)

If Grace had not participated in her company 401(k) plan, she would have earned $30,000 and paid about $4,000 in federal taxes for net earnings of $26,000. Because of her participation, instead of having zero savings, she has $2,700 (plus earnings) in her 401(k) account. Because her W-2 earnings are only $28,200 instead of $30,000, her federal income taxes are about $270 less than she would have paid if she had not participated in her plan.

Age Considerations

No matter what your age, if you are working and eligible for a 401(k) plan or other tax-deferred company plan, do not pass it up without careful consideration. Certainly most people under 65 should normally participate to the maximum permitted by the plan. Even if you are 70, the plan may still be worth it, especially if you have a match or profit-sharing contribution. Yes, "70." If you are still employed after 70, you are still eligible to contribute and participate in the benefits of your employer's 401(k), 403(b), or 457 plan.

Traditional IRA

The Individual Retirement Account was enacted by Congress in 1974 (effective 1975) to give tax incentives to individuals to encourage them to save for their retirement. At one time, everyone who qualified for an IRA could deduct the contribution from income for tax purposes. Later, in 1981, Congress placed income limits on deduction eligibility, but broadened the number of people who could qualify for an IRA.

> **TIP**
>
> No matter what your age, if you are working and eligible for a 401(k) plan or other tax-deferred company plan, do not pass it up without careful consideration.

Recently (in 1997 and 1998), Congress liberalized deductibility and made other enhancements to the IRA, including the creation of a number of different types of IRAs, such as the Roth IRA (see Chapter 27).

Anyone under the age of 70½ who earns income is eligible for a traditional Individual Retirement Account (IRA), even if he participates in a 401(k), 403(b), 457 plan, or SEP. The maximum you can contribute to a traditional IRA is only $2,000 each year and that is one of its limitations.

Whether you can take a tax deduction for your contribution will depend on the circumstances. If you do not participate in your company's 401(k) plan or pension plan, you can deduct the full amount of your contribution on your income tax return. The deduction goes on line 23 of your Form 1040 as an adjustment to income. Since the deduction effectively reduces the amount of taxable income, it has the same effect on your taxes as a pretax contribution to your company's 401(k) account.

If your company does not offer a 401(k) plan, a traditional IRA is a good idea. Even though you won't be getting a matching contribution from anyone, you will be getting the advantages of tax-deferred investing and pretax contributions, if you qualify.

You may be able to get a tax deduction for your IRA contribution even if you do participate in your company's retirement plan. This depends on your annual income. For example, if you are single with an adjusted gross income of $33,000 or less, you are eligible for the full deduction for tax year 2001. If you are married filing a joint return, you are eligible if your adjusted gross income is $53,000 or less. Single individuals with adjusted gross incomes of $43,000 or more are not eligible for a deduction for tax year 2001. Neither are married couples filing jointly with adjusted gross incomes of $63,000 or more. For tax years after 2001, these limits increase annually to 2005. To check the applicable limits, see IRS Publication 590.

Traditional IRAs allow tax deferral until you take your money out. You are required to begin withdrawing funds from your IRA after the age of 70½. This is true of your tax-deferred company savings plan as well, unless you are still employed by the company offering the plan.

> **NOTE**
>
> Taking advantage of the traditional IRA each year will effectively get you pretax savings as well as tax-deferral advantages.

If you begin withdrawals before age 59½, usually a 10 percent penalty is payable to the IRS. This is also true for 401(k) accounts in most cases. First-time home purchasers can avoid the penalty for a withdrawal of up to $10,000 from a traditional IRA. Many people borrow from their 401(k) accounts for this purpose.

You can set up an IRA account at most brokerage firms, mutual funds, and banks. They will provide the forms you need. You choose the investments. There is generally a nominal fee of perhaps $10 a year for the maintenance of the account.

The traditional IRA is limited in its ability to make a big impact for many people due to the low contribution limit of $2,000 per year. And, many people do not qualify for the deduction.

But let's say your company does not offer a 401(k) plan or other retirement plan. Taking advantage of the traditional IRA each year will effectively get you pretax savings as well as tax-deferral advantages. Although limited in amount, this is still worth having, particularly for younger individuals who have time on their side.

What the traditional IRA will not get you is the benefit of a company matching contribution that a 401(k) plan can offer. Even if you qualify for a tax deduction on a traditional IRA, check out your company 401(k) plan first. You don't want to be passing up a company matching contribution. If you don't qualify for a tax-deductible IRA or a Roth, consider a nondeductible IRA that allows you to defer $2,000 a year in after-tax dollars and to generate tax-deferred growth.

Tax-Deferred Variable Annuity

To encourage people to save for retirement, variable annuities have received favorable tax treatment since the 1950s. Variable annuities are tax-deferred investments that combine an investment feature with a life insurance policy and an annuity feature. You can think of the modern-day tax deferred variable annuity as a collection of tax-deferred managed funds (similar to mutual funds) that allow you to invest on a tax-deferred basis in one investment for multiple objectives. The life insurance policy provides a death benefit usually in the amount of your purchase price, which can increase in amount over time if the policy so provides. The annuity feature is something you can use or ignore. Essentially, by annuitizing you opt to turn over your investment in the product to the insurance company that sponsors it in return for a promise to pay you a certain sum of money for the rest of your life. There are many variations on the theme in terms of the selection of investments made available through the product, the insurance features, and the annuitization features. In addition, since the insurance industry perceives the variable annuity to be the answer to every baby boomer's wishes, we are seeing many innovations to the product that make it more and more desirable.

> **NOTE**
>
> Variable annuities are tax-deferred investments that combine an investment feature with a life insurance policy and an annuity feature.

If understood, tax-deferred variable annuities can be particularly valuable to people with inadequate retirement resources. This is especially true if someone has an investment horizon of 10 years or longer and few or no retirement assets or benefits. You need to understand how this investment works, however, and must be particularly careful to consider the downside before buying a variable annuity.

These annuities offer investors a way to "buy" tax deferral above the $2,000 annual limit on IRAs imposed by the IRS. The IRS sets no limits on how much you can put aside into a tax-deferred variable annuity. So, you can buy as much as you want.

Investments are tax-deferred much like an IRA. That means that you do not pay taxes on any gains you may realize within the annuity when you sell one annuity investment option and replace it with another. Nor, do you pay any income taxes on any earnings during that time.

You pay taxes when you make a withdrawal from the annuity at ordinary income tax rates, not capital gains tax rates, which is comparable to the tax treatment of other tax-deferred accounts such as traditional IRAs. There are no taxes on the amount you originally invested. Since Congress intended tax-deferred variable annuities as retirement vehicles, there are penalties for early withdrawal before age 59½ similar to those for the IRA. If you have a large net worth, do be sure to understand the estate tax and income tax consequences of owning a sizable annuity.

What You Need to Know before You Buy

Misunderstandings between the investor and the salesman can cast a shadow over any investment. But certain products seem to attract more than their share of confusion. Variable annuities fall into this category, probably because the product can be complicated and easily misunderstood. For example, the insurance part of the policy may be understood as a "guarantee" against investment losses. The problem is that in most cases, you have to die to claim this benefit.

Usually, you can protect yourself from harm by reading the prospectus and application carefully. The students in my continuing education classes tell me it is hard enough to read a 10-page mutual fund prospectus. Variable annuity prospectuses can be 100 pages long and dull enough to put you to sleep. The prospectus has two parts. One deals with how the annuity itself works. The other deals with the separate accounts, which are the investments offered by the annuity. In the prospectus, you will find a discussion of any "guarantees" the salesperson may mention; how death benefits work; how annuity payments may work; and costs, penalties, and risks, among other things. Be absolutely certain to read this prospectus before you invest any money. This is not a time to rely on what you think you heard. You need to see it in writing, since you will not be able to get out of most variable annuities without severe penalties.

In my practice, if I come across a situation in which a client might benefit from a variable annuity, I like to ask him to fill out a questionnaire that he would only be able to answer if he did in fact read the

> **NOTE**
> If understood, tax-deferred variable annuities can be particularly valuable to people with inadequate retirement resources.

prospectus. If the client is willing to fill out the questionnaire, then I'm willing to discuss things further.

If you focus on risks, costs, and taxes, that will take you a long way. You need to understand the following five things at a minimum:

1. How much is taken out of your investment when you invest? If the answer is zero, that does not mean your salesperson makes nothing on the sale. In fact, variable annuity sales are quite lucrative to salespeople.

2. If your salesperson does not disclose his commission to you on his own, ask him what he will be paid if you go ahead with the purchase. You always want to know if the commission is the reason behind the recommendation.

3. How much is deducted from the value of your investment if you need to take out money in three months, one year, three years, and so on? Usually, annuities provide for contingent deferred sales charges if you withdraw your money soon after any investment.

4. What are the income and estate tax consequences when you withdraw funds?

5. What are the ongoing costs of owning the annuity? You will need to understand the total operating costs of the investment vehicles separate from the cost of the annuity.

Summary

You may think that tax-deferred accounts only benefit younger investors. That is not the case. If you have the opportunity to participate in a tax-deferred company plan that features an employer contribution, take advantage of it no matter how old you are, even after age 70 if you qualify. At 50 to 65 or so, most people will benefit from building up their tax-deferred retirement accounts as much as possible. Only the very wealthy may not wish to do so, if their tax-deferred plans already contain sizable assets. As to how to invest these accounts, that will depend on where you are in your investment life cycle, as discussed in Chapter 8.

CHAPTER 27

Roth IRAs

The Roth IRA is a new type of IRA created by Congress as part of the 1997 Taxpayer Relief Act. What is exciting about a Roth is that it is a tax-free IRA, instead of a tax-deferred IRA.

Features of the Roth IRA

The Roth IRA is different from the rest. No contribution to a Roth IRA is *tax deductible*. And, no qualified withdrawal from a Roth IRA is *taxable*. Assuming you meet the requirements, which I discuss below, any contribution you make to a Roth IRA can be invested for growth or income or both without ever generating a tax bill.

Moreover, you can keep your Roth IRA intact for as long as you like. Unlike a traditional IRA, there is no IRS requirement to begin withdrawals when you reach a certain age (70½ or later if still employed). That is, the mandatory distribution requirements of the traditional IRA that trigger withdrawals—and taxes—do not apply to the Roth IRA.

TAX-FREE INCOME AND TAX-FREE GROWTH

In essence, the Roth IRA gives you the opportunity to invest for growth or for income or both on a tax-free basis. There are withdrawal restrictions such as the 10 percent IRS penalty for early withdrawal that applies under age 59½. In addition, you generally have to wait five years after conversion to take out earnings tax-free. (See "The Five-Year Rule" below.) All qualified distributions are tax-free.

Considering the nature of the investment enterprise, and assuming you meet the qualifications, the Roth IRA gives you a chance to create your own source of *tax-free income* as well as your own source of *tax-free growth*. And, this is the reason people are opening Roth IRA's if they can.

Everyone who qualifies, irrespective of age, should consider a Roth. Qualification depends on how much you make.

DO YOU QUALIFY?

Generally, if you are single, you can contribute up to $2,000 to your Roth IRA if your modified adjusted gross income is $95,000 or less. The same amount applies to heads of households and persons married filing separately if they did not live with the spouse at any time during the year.

Generally, if you are married filing a joint return, you can contribute up to $2,000 if your modified adjusted gross income is $150,000 or less. If you make more than these amounts, you may still be able to contribute some amount less than the full $2,000 each year. Check with your accountant to be sure.

MAXIMUM CONTRIBUTIONS

The Roth IRA would be a panacea for investors trying to save for retirement but for one significant limitation. The maximum you can contribute to a Roth IRA is $2,000 per year. However, if you qualify, it may be possible to convert another IRA to a Roth IRA.

NOTE

Unlike the traditional IRA and the 401(k), there are no mandatory distribution requirements to contend with after age 70½.

Conversion

Depending on how much you make, you may be eligible to convert all or part of your traditional IRA account to a Roth IRA. Since there are some advantages to converting, it is a good idea to check with your tax adviser on eligibility. You are eligible to convert even if you participate in a company retirement plan.

CONVERSION QUALIFICATIONS

Whether you can convert your IRA into a Roth IRA depends on your earnings. Generally by law, you may not earn more than $100,000 in the year of conversion. The $100,000 limit is your modified adjusted gross income. That's your adjusted gross income from your tax return, decreased by certain deductions such as adoption expenses and series EE bond interest.

WHY CONVERT?

If you meet the conversion qualifications described above, you can turn your tax-deferred IRA into a tax-free IRA. What's your potential reward? No taxes on qualified distributions, ever. At what price? You have to pay taxes at the time of conversion.

HERE IS HOW CONVERSION WORKS

Say you are 50 years old. Last year when you changed jobs, you set up a rollover IRA with your 401(k) account from your previous employer. Now, you have $200,000 in your rollover IRA and you want to convert it to a Roth. Your accountant determines that you qualify for a conversion. You contact your broker or investment adviser and tell him that you would like to convert your IRA to a Roth IRA. You receive an application with an authorization to transfer $200,000 from your IRA to a new Roth IRA in your name.

NOTE

The mandatory distribution requirements of the traditional IRA that trigger withdrawals—and taxes—do not apply to the Roth IRA.

The monies that are withdrawn from your old IRA become taxable as a distribution. Because they are being transferred into a Roth IRA, no early withdrawal penalty is due even though you are under the age of 59½.

THE FIVE-YEAR RULE

As mentioned, to be tax-free, the distribution from a Roth IRA must be *qualified*. If a distribution is qualified, it is not included in your gross income. Once you convert, only your earnings or growth could be taxable, since you have already paid taxes on the principal. For example, assume you convert $200,000 from a traditional IRA into a Roth. If the account grows to $300,000 in four years and you want to withdraw all $300,000, the $100,000 growth may be taxable. You would have to wait five years for the entire account to be tax-free. If you wait until after age 59½, it will also be penalty-free.

There are exceptions to the five-year rule. If you become disabled or buy your first home, for example, your distribution is qualified as tax-free even if you don't wait five years. For more information on the Roth IRA, see IRS Publication 553 (Highlights of 1997 Tax Changes) and IRS Publication 590 (IRAs), which you may obtain from the IRS by calling 800-TAX-FORM.

Summary

I strongly believe that anyone who meets the income qualifications should set up a Roth IRA, whether or not he has other tax deferred accounts such as traditional IRA's or 401(k) accounts offered at work. Converting an existing IRA to a Roth is another matter.

To determine whether you are a good candidate for a Roth IRA *conversion*, you must look at your holdings, your age, other retirement assets, and your potential tax bite. And, bring your accountant into the loop well before you make your decision.

If you are trying to decide between a Roth and contributing to a 401(k) at work, it is best to do both if at all possible.

The Roth IRA is nondeductible under all circumstances. That means that the Roth is always made with after-tax dollars as opposed to pretax dollars. For that reason, your compounding potential will not be as great as with your company 401(k) plan if it offers a matching contribution. But, the Roth IRA also has one big advantage. If you meet certain requirements, a Roth IRA is never taxed, even when you take your money out. To reiterate, generally, if you keep your money in a Roth IRA for at least five years and you are age 59½ or older, you can withdraw everything, even the growth and the income, without any tax consequences. None of your growth or earnings are taxed at any time if you meet these requirements. Unlike the traditional IRA and the 401(k), there are no mandatory distribution requirements to contend with after age 70½. And, you can continue contributing to your Roth IRA even after the age of 70½.

Contributions to a Roth IRA can be withdrawn at any time without penalty because your investments are made in after-tax monies. Earnings you receive in your Roth may be subject to taxes and penalties, depending on your age and length of holding period. As with the traditional IRA—but only after five years—you can withdraw up to $10,000 for the purchase of a first home without penalty or tax. The penalty will not apply even if you are under the age of 59½.

Remember, the Roth is not tax-deferred. It is tax-free. In contrast to a traditional IRA, you will not get a tax bill from Uncle Sam when you take out your Roth money in retirement.

CHAPTER 28

Timing Mandatory Distributions after Age 70½

Age 70½ is an important turning point. It signals the time to start withdrawing money from your tax-deferred savings accounts, such as your traditional IRA, 401(k), or 403(b) (but not your Roth IRA, as discussed in Chapter 27). The U.S. Treasury has been foregoing income and capital gains taxes on these accounts for a long time. At this point, the law says that you must begin taking money out, which in turn triggers a taxable distribution. These legally mandated withdrawals are called mandatory distributions. If you fail to take out the required minimum amount each year, there are severe penalties.

Until recent changes in the law that became effective in 2001, making the right withdrawal decisions was far from easy. You could choose different methods for calculating the mandatory distribution, including methods called *recalculating*, *nonrecalculating*, or *term certain* and *hybrid* methods. These terms no longer apply. We'll go through how to calculate mandatory distributions under the new rules in Chapter 29. In this chapter, let's tackle the issue of timing.

There is quite a bit of confusion about when you've hit the date that triggers mandatory distributions. It is important to know the correct date that applies in your situation, since missing a withdrawal can cost you money. If you do not start to take money out as required by law, there is a severe penalty. You must pay the IRS a penalty of 50 percent of the amount that you needed to withdraw but did not.

Age

Let me illustrate the age trigger with a few examples. Let's look at three people who reach age 70 in the same year. You need to know when they reach 70½ in order to figure out when the withdrawals must begin. Let's suppose it is the year 2001. Mary's birthday is May 31, 1931. John's birthday is January 1, 1931. Bill's birthday is August 4, 1931. You need to know when each of them reaches the age of 70½.

The June 30 Rule

Here is an easy way to calculate when someone reaches age 70½. If your birthday is between January 1st and June 30th, you will reach 70½ in the year you celebrate your seventieth birthday. If your birthday is between June 30 and December 31, you will reach 70½ in the year of your seventy-first birthday. Since John and Mary's birthdays are before June 30, they are 70½ in the year 2001. But Bill's birthday is after June 30, so he isn't 70½ until 2002.

Mandatory Distributions

The mandatory distribution rules come into play in the year you reach 70½. So, in this example, Mary and John must make their IRA withdrawal decisions before December 31, 2001. Bill can wait until 2002 to make his mandatory distribution decisions.

Two decisions will need to be made, timing and method of calculating withdrawals.

Timing Decision

The first decision Mary and John have to make has to do with the timing of their first mandatory distribution. They each can decide to take their first distribution anytime in the year 2001 or they can each wait until anytime before April 1, 2002. The April 1 date is Mary and John's "required beginning date." Since Bill doesn't reach age 70½ until 2002, his required beginning date is April 1, 2003. Required beginning date is defined in IRS Publication 590, which I recommend to anyone who has a tax deferred account. Publication 590 is available at no cost by calling the IRS at 800-TAX-FORM. You can also find the publication online at www.irs.gov.

Let me give you the legal background on this rule and then explain the consequences of waiting until your required beginning date to take your first mandatory distribution.

The law allows Mary and John, who both reached the age of 70½ in the year 2001, to take their first required minimum distribution anytime before December 31, 2001, *or* to delay that year's distribution to any time before April 1 of the following year, in this case, 2002. Some people would opt for waiting until April 1, 2002, but there is a reason not to wait in certain circumstances. Let me show you.

Let's say Mary decides to take her distribution before December 31, 2001, and John decides to wait until April 1, 2002. For this example, both have $100,000 in their IRA accounts on December 31, 2000. And, let's assume that in the year 2001, each of their IRA accounts grows by 8 percent.

Using the formula that applies in her case, Mary will take out $3,817 sometime in 2001 as her first mandatory distribution based on a December 31, 2000, value of $100,000, even though she can legally delay taking this money out until April 1 of the following year. Because she takes the withdrawal in 2001, the distribution will be fully taxed as income on her 2001 tax return (unless the IRA was funded with after-tax contributions). In the year 2002, Mary will take out another distribution of $4,118, based on a December 31, 2001, value of $104,183, which includes our assumed growth of 8 percent less the first mandatory withdrawal. That distribution will be taxed as income on her 2002 tax return.

> **TIP**
>
> "Required beginning date" is defined in IRS Publication 590. Publication 590 is available free by calling the IRS at 800-TAX-FORM.

Compare John's situation. He has the same amount of money in his IRA as of December 31, 2000 ($100,000), and also earns 8 percent in 2001. In contrast to Mary, he decides to delay his first mandatory distribution to *April 1, 2002, his (and Mary's) required beginning date.*

Since John is not taking any distribution in 2001, he has no income to report with respect to his IRA on his year 2001 Form 1040 tax return. The April 1 distribution is John's year 2001 mandatory distribution, which the IRS permits you to delay to the year 2002 in this example. But the IRS does *NOT* permit you to delay your next mandatory distribution. That means that you still have to take your year 2002 distribution in the year 2002, anytime before December 31, 2002.

Since he is waiting until April 1, 2002, to take his $3,817 mandatory distribution, he will have to take two mandatory distributions in the year 2002—the $3,817 mandatory distribution in 2001 and a distribution of $4,269 in 2002. He will have to report both IRA distributions totaling $8,085 on his 2002 tax return.

BILL

Since Bill is not 70½ until the year 2002, his mandatory distribution in the year 2001 is zero. He will be in Mary and John's position in the year 2002, not 2001.

Method of Calculating Withdrawals

Until changes in the law in 2001, there were three different methods to figure withdrawals, the term certain method or nonrecalculating method, the recalculating method, and a hybrid method. Now, for the majority of people, there is a single method of calculating withdrawals under the New Uniform Life Expectancy Table, which I discuss in Chapter 29. It makes life much easier. Since the method of calculation is the same for everyone who is the same age, you no longer need to wonder if you are using the best method for your situation.

NOTE

It is important to take responsibility for mandatory distributions because of the penalties that apply if you don't.

Summary

Age 70½ is an important time. Knowing when to start mandatory distributions from your IRA can be a little tricky, as is calculating the minimum required by law. It is important to take responsibility for mandatory distributions because of the penalties that apply if you don't. The IRS assesses a penalty of 50 percent on the amount that should have been, but was not withdrawn. If you are approaching age 70½ or if you have a parent or relative who is, it may be helpful to you to read more about mandatory distributions. To see how mandatory distribution planning might work in a real-life situation, I provide a case study in Chapter 29. For additional resources, see the Appendix.

Mandatory Distribution Planning

IRA distribution planning is a topic that is already stirring controversy, as I saw in a recent 401(k) presentation I gave at the *Boston Globe*'s Personal Finance Conference and Expo. Drawing readers of all ages and walks of life, distribution planning generated the greatest number of questions in my session and it continues to be one of the more popular questions I get from readers of my weekly column. IRA distribution planning has to do with not only how to calculate mandatory distributions wisely, but also how to pass tax deferral on to younger generations.

This chapter provides a case study that illustrates how distribution planning might work for a retired couple with a substantial IRA.

Jim and Mary's Assets

Mary, whose birthday is January 1, 1931, is 70½ in 2001. She wants to know how to fill out the mandatory withdrawal form she just received from her IRA custodian, a well-known company that sells mutual funds directly to investors through the mail.

Mary has been married to Jim, age 74, for 50 years. They have four grown children, each with children of their own. Jim has a small Individual Retirement Account (IRA) of $40,000. He also has $140,000 in a taxable account.

Mary has a larger IRA of $500,000 from which she needs to begin mandatory distributions in the year 2001 or at the latest, April 1 of the year 2002 (her required beginning date). This is the largest asset held by the couple, along with their house, which is also valued at $500,000 and is held in their joint names.

In lieu of Social Security, Mary receives a teacher's pension of $37,000, which increases each year due to an annual cost-of-living adjustment. To get a higher pension, Mary elected to take a single instead of a joint and survivor pension when she retired. Jim receives a Social Security pension of $14,000 a year. Social Security retirement benefits also increase each year to offset inflation. Together with Mary's pension, that gives the couple $51,000 a year, which is enough to cover living expenses.

In addition, Mary will receive $260,000 as an insurance death benefit if Jim predeceases her. And, she has $120,000 in a taxable account. Mary's Will names Jim as her sole beneficiary, and his Will names her as his sole beneficiary.

NOTE

IRA distribution planning has to do with not only how to calculate mandatory distributions wisely, but also how to pass tax deferral on to younger generations.

Meeting Mary's Needs

Mary wants to keep her taxes as low as possible and at death, leave her IRA to her four children. Before the release of the proposed Treasury regulations in January 2001 that changed the method of calculating distributions, the name of the game was to try to reduce distributions and lengthen the distribution period. There were a number of ways to accomplish this result, many of them complicated. Since many of you may have arrangements put in place under the old law, I want to illustrate those methods first and then compare the new law. But, I caution you against making any changes in your own situation before speaking with your tax adviser.

Under the old law, Mary might have been advised to split her $500,000 IRA into four $125,000 IRAs. She would have named each of her four children as a joint life beneficiary along with herself and elected the term certain method of distribution. On the Required

Minimum Distribution Form, that would have meant checking the term certain method of life expectancy calculation, along with a box that says "my beneficiary is not my spouse." The term certain method was one of two methods allowed by the IRS to spread out mandatory distribution payments over the IRA owner's life expectancy.

Since the children were nonspouse beneficiaries who are more than 10 years younger than Mary, she would have used the 10-year table (MDIB table) to figure her annual required distributions. MDIB is the term that applies when the owner designates a nonspouse beneficiary who was more than 10 years younger than the IRA owner, in this case Mary. Under the tables, the law permitted no more than a 10-year differential between the owner and the nonspouse beneficiary for purposes of the calculation. That is, even if the nonspouse beneficiary was 20 or 30 years younger, the taxpayer only got the benefit of 10 years. The MDIB table is found in Appendix E of IRS Publication 590, which is available by calling 800-TAX-FORM. This publication is essential reading for anyone who has an IRA and includes all the definitions and the distribution methods.

If you did the calculation in accordance with the formula in the table, Mary would be withdrawing a total of $19,083.97 ($500,000 divided by 26.2) in her first mandatory distribution. This would be substantially less than she would have needed to withdraw if she had used her husband (who is age 74) as a joint life beneficiary, which would have come to $24,752.48 ($500,000 divided by 20.2). Thus, you can see the benefit of using the MDIB tables, something you could generally only do under the old law if you named your children as your designated beneficiaries.

After Mary's death, each child would have been able to continue taking distributions based on his own life expectancy, which would allow the continued build up of the IRA over a much longer time frame. Under the new regulations, there are no term certain or recalculating elections. Instead there is a single uniform table, whose divisors are the same as the old MDIB table. Thus, there is no longer any need to name a young beneficiary. Now, any IRA owner can use the tax-advantaged MDIB tables (now called the Uniform Table) irrespective of the age of your beneficiary.

In this case, since the uniform table is based on the MDIB table, Mary's first mandatory withdrawal would be the same under the new law as under the old law, but Mary would not need to name her children to take advantage of the table. She could name her husband, Jim, and still have the same result. That is, the divisor in the Uniform Table is 26.2 and Mary's first mandatory withdrawal would be $19,083.97 ($500,000 divided by 26.2).

As under the old law, after Mary's death, each child would have been able to continue taking distributions based on his own life expectancy under the single life tables (Table 1 in Appendix E of Publication 590), which would allow the continued tax-deferred build up of the IRA over the lives of each child as beneficiary of each of Mary's IRAs.

New Problem

Under the old law, Mary would have been able to lower her mandatory distributions by naming her children instead of Jim as designated beneficiaries. But this solution would have created a big problem lurking beneath the surface. What would have happened if Mary predeceased Jim?

Even though Jim was named in Mary's Will as her sole beneficiary, he would have had no claim to Mary's IRA, which would have gone directly to her children due to the IRA beneficiary designations. His only assets would be the house, Mary's taxable account of $120,000, and his own IRA and taxable account. Since Mary's pension of $37,000 terminates at her death, Jim's income would have dropped to $14,000 a year. This was a far cry from the $51,000 he needed for living expenses.

Protecting Jim If Mary Dies First

Under the old law, Mary's tax advisers would have recommended a convoluted solution to protect Jim while keeping mandatory distributions and taxes to a minimum.

Beneficiary Designation

To protect Jim's interests if Mary died before he did, Mary needed to name her husband, Jim, as her "designated" beneficiary, instead of their four children, who would be named as "contingent" beneficiaries. These terms appear on Mary's IRA distribution form. You'll get a better understanding of what they mean as you see how they are used.

Briefly, a designated beneficiary is an IRS term used to mean the person who you name on your IRA distribution form to serve two purposes: to receive your IRA when you die and to serve as a measuring life for distribution purposes. A contingent beneficiary is the

EXAMPLE   **175**

person who inherits the IRA if the designated beneficiary dies before the owner. In this case, as the designated beneficiary, if Jim predeceased Mary, her IRA would go to her four children who are her contingent beneficiaries.

That part is relatively easy. Choosing the distribution method requires thinking through what happens when either spouse dies before the other. This is where complications set in under the old method.

Distribution Method

Under the old law, the IRA distribution form that Mary needed to fill out and return to her IRA custodian gave her two distribution methods: term certain and recalculation. Under the term certain method, a set number of years was used to distribute the entire IRA. Under the recalculation method, the IRA was distributed throughout the owner's life.

In Mary's case, experts would have recommended a complicated "hybrid" method of distribution planning. Hybrid was a term that was not used by the Internal Revenue Code (Code) or the tax regulations, however. To use this method, Mary would have needed to attach a distribution instruction to her distribution form, since hybrid was not an option listed on the form.

Example

Jim was born in 1927 and Mary was born in 1931. Mary's IRA was valued at $500,000 on December 31, 2000. Mary's life expectancy could have been recalculated and a form of term certain method known as the "adjusted age calculation" could have been used in respect of Jim's life expectancy.

Using the hybrid method with Mary recalculating and Jim's life expectancy not recalculating, the first year's divisor was 19.4 years and the required distribution was $25,773.20. (Joint life expectancy table in Appendix E of IRS Publication 590.) This was the best Jim and Mary could do under the old rules with Jim as the designated beneficiary. Under the new rules, the divisor is the more favorable 26.2 years, as discussed before.

Under the old rules, if Jim's life had been recalculated, and he died before Mary, she would have had to shorten her withdrawal period. This was due to the fact that at death, Jim's life expectancy went to zero under the recalculating method. That would have left Mary with having to use the single life expectancy table for her mandatory distributions going forward. The single table required greater distributions taken more quickly, and thus more taxes. That is the reason the adviser would have recommended the hybrid method. That is, under the hybrid method just discussed, if Jim died first, Mary continued to use the joint life expectancy method for distributions after his death, which would have been better than the single life tables required to be used if Jim's life were also recalculated.

Under the new regulations, there is no hybrid method, no recalculating method, no term certain method, and no need to find creative ways to lower distributions. Instead, Mary would simply use the Uniform Table and divide by 26.2 for her first distribution, irrespective of whether she named Jim or her children as designated beneficiary. That is a big improvement over the old rules and helps simplify taxpayers' lives considerably.

Under the new regulations, if Jim dies first, Mary can simply change the designated beneficiary. It was not possible under the old law to change the designated beneficiary so as to increase the distribution period. Under the new regulations, the designated beneficiary can be changed any time up to the date of death of the IRA owner and even up to the last day of the calendar year following the year of death, through the use of beneficiary disclaimers. A disclaimer is a way for a beneficiary to voluntarily decline taking an interest in the IRA.

Mary Dies—Jim Inherits

Under both the old and the new regulations, if Jim lives longer than Mary, as Mary's designated beneficiary, Jim will inherit Mary's IRA. He will be able to roll over Mary's IRA into an IRA he sets up in his own name if he wishes or he can leave it intact, which may be a benefit since he is older than Mary. That is, the inherited IRA can continue distributions under Mary's schedule, assuming her life expectancy under the Uniform Table. For example, if Mary were 80 at her death, her divisor would be 17.6 compared to 14.5 for Jim, who is 4 years older.

If Jim had transferred the inherited IRA to his own name, he could have named new designated beneficiaries and elected a brand new distribution program. Jim needs to do this before December 31 of the year following the year of Mary's death. Jim would have use of the IRA for his lifetime and would be able to pass along unused portions to the four children.

Under the old regulations, Jim would have been advised to split his inherited IRA into four new IRAs in his name, one for each of his children as designated beneficiaries. From then on, the minimum

EXAMPLE **177**

distribution incidental benefit (MDIB) tables would have applied to determine the required distribution. Let's say Jim was 73 at the time he made this arrangement. One IRA listed his daughter, Joan, as designated beneficiary. Joan was born in 1951. Using the MDIB Tables, the divisor at the owner's age of 73 would have been 23.5 years for a distribution of $5,319.15 assuming a $125,000 balance on December 31 of the prior year. Each of the three remaining IRAs for the other children would have been set up the same way.

Jim Dies—Joan Inherits

Under the old rules, at Jim's death, each child would have had the ability to continue tax-deferred growth based on the remaining actual joint life expectancy, which allowed the IRA to last longer than it would have if Jim had not set up a new IRA with Mary's inherited IRA.

Under the new laws, after the death of the owner (Jim), the child beneficiary (Joan) goes to the single life tables and starts taking distributions under her life expectancy.

Joan's IRA Inherited from Jim

Importantly, Joan needs to understand that she should not "re-title" the IRA she inherits from Jim into her own name. She should keep the IRA in the name of Jim, and it should be noted as an inherited IRA with her Social Security number added to it.

Here's why. If she walks into a bank, brokerage firm, or mutual fund distributor and asks them to transfer or re-title her father's IRA into her own name, a little known but very painful IRS rule steps in to cause a full and immediate taxable distribution of the IRA. If Jim's IRA is worth $125,000 at the time, she will get a 1099-R from the bank indicating that she earned $125,000 of income that year, all of which is taxable.

Under some IRA custodian arrangements, Joan may be able to deal with the inherited IRA as her own in the sense that she may designate her own beneficiary. Each plan must be checked to determine if this is allowed and by what method. Some may allow it with a designated beneficiary form or some may require it in a Will.

Joan Dies

If Joan names her son as the beneficiary of the inherited IRA, he inherits the right to her IRA funds at her death, if allowed by the IRA custodial agreement. The IRA will still be titled in the name of Jim, Inherited IRA, Joan's son as beneficiary, under the son's Social Security number. He would continue Joan's schedule of withdrawals as if he stood in her shoes.

Summary

As you can see from this simple fact pattern, IRA distribution planning can be hair-raising. Smaller IRAs in the tens of thousands are not going to be affected that much. But larger IRAs will. The new laws effective in 2001 help simplify things somewhat. They eliminate the need to choose distribution methodologies, since everyone—with one exception (spouses more than 10 years younger)—uses the same table, the Uniform Table, which is based on the old MDIB table. No matter who your beneficiary is, if you are 70½, your divisor is 26.2. If you are 75, your divisor is 21.8. All you need to do is look up your age in the table to check your divisor. The table allows distributions to be taken out over a lifetime, as opposed to stopping at a certain age.

What the new regulations do not do, however, is remove or reduce the substantial 50 percent penalty to withdraw the appropriate minimum required distribution on an annual basis. The IRA will still have to be implemented as part of your estate plan. So, planning is a must. Take my advice. Don't wait until age 70 to start putting together a team of trusted advisers who will be able to help you plan your distributions. Even with the new changes in the law, what may seem relatively straightforward can touch multiple generations.

CHAPTER 30

Social Security

As you approach retirement, you need to make decisions with respect to your Social Security retirement benefits. Because of the nuances to Social Security qualification and the variety of benefits, I highly recommend that you take some time to understand the options available to you personally.

The Social Security Administration provides many resources to help you, including personal calculators that you can use on the Social Security Web site. The Web address is www.ssa.gov. In addition, the Social Security Administration encourages members of the public to contact them for personal assistance, including what-if scenarios that would help you decide which options are best for you. In this chapter, let's talk about retirement benefits, spouse benefits, and survivor benefits.

Retirement Benefits

If you were born before 1938, your full retirement age is 65. If you were born in 1960 or later, your full retirement age is 67. If you were born between 1960 and 1938, your full retirement age is between 65 and 67.

No matter when your full retirement benefits start, you have the option of taking early retirement benefits as early as 62, but your benefit will be lower than if you were to wait until your full retirement date. According to Social Security, early retirement benefits will equal full retirement benefits, when added together over your life expectancy. If you delay payment until age 70, your monthly benefits will be greater than if you retire earlier.

Early Retirement versus Full Retirement Age

The actual dollar amount of your monthly Social Security retirement benefit will vary based on how long you worked and how much you contributed to Social Security. In addition, you may be eligible for retirement benefits indirectly, for example, through a spouse or former spouse if you are divorced or widowed.

Spousal Benefits

Even if you were never employed, if your spouse qualifies for benefits, you may also qualify for a Social Security retirement benefit check of your own. Generally, you will receive up to one half of your spouse's benefit, even if you did not work and even if your spouse is currently receiving his or her own Social Security check. To qualify for spousal retirement benefits, you and your spouse must both be at least 62 years old.

Survivor Benefits

If you are married and both you and your spouse contributed to Social Security, you may be eligible for a higher survivor's benefit. Let me illustrate. Annie, age 70, receives a $400 monthly spousal benefit from Social Security and her husband, George, receives $1,176. What would happen to Annie if she outlives George? Due to special benefits for the widowed, Annie will receive George's $1,176 benefit instead of her $400 spousal benefit. The amount of a survivor's benefit depends on your age and on what your spouse received or was eligible to receive at the time of death.

If you are 65 or older, as in Annie's case, you will receive 100 percent of your spouse's benefit. At age 60, the benefit is 71½ percent of your spouse's benefit. If you are disabled, as defined by Social Security, the benefit can start as early as age 50.

According to a spokesperson for the Social Security Administration, when the agency learns of the death of your spouse, what happens next depends on whether you are receiving a spousal benefit like Annie's. Since Annie is receiving spousal benefits and is over age 65, she will receive a notice from Social Security telling her the revised benefit she will be getting, and the effective date of the revision. In Annie's case, she will also receive a $255 death benefit, which is payable to surviving spouses who have the same address as the decedent.

If you are not receiving a spousal benefit from Social Security, you will get a letter advising you to contact the local Social Security office about possible survivor benefits.

To ensure that Social Security is aware of the death, it is best for the surviving spouse or a family member to call Social Security to make sure that they receive notification of death. You can call the national office at 800-772-1213 from 7 A.M. to 7 P.M. for this purpose. Or, to speak to a local office, you can call the same 800-number and press option 5. After you enter your zip code, you will be given the location and phone number for your local Social Security office.

◤NOTE

According to Social Security, early retirement benefits will equal full retirement benefits, when added together over your life expectancy.

When you call, you will need the name of the decedent and his or her Social Security number and address. You will also need to know if benefits were being sent by mail, or deposited electronically to the decedent's bank account.

Social Security will need to see some documents to establish the surviving spouses age and marital status. Preferred proofs of age are a birth certificate or religious record recorded before you were five years of age. Documents must be original or certified copies. Photocopies are not acceptable. You will not be able to use a driver's license or a passport.

It is important to be timely in notifying the Social Security office of the death, since waiting can cause complications. For example, if you and your spouse were both receiving benefits, you may receive two checks for a time when you are only due one. In that case, you may need to repay amounts that were not due you.

If your spouse did not receive any benefits before death, you will need to apply for survivor's benefits before any payments are sent to you. Do not delay. Payments are not retroactive to the date of death.

Finally, you may be due a survivor's benefit even if you are divorced. If you were married for 10 years, you can make application for a survivor's benefit by phone. You will need to supply supporting documentation, such as a marriage certificate and a record of the divorce.

Summary

Social Security benefits can play an important part in your retirement planning. It makes sense to take an active role in understanding what they will be and to make sure you don't overlook benefits due to you in the event of divorce or death.

For more information on survivor's benefits, I highly recommend you read two booklets you can obtain from Social Security at no charge. They are called "Social Security: What Every Woman Should Know" and "Social Security: Survivor's Benefits." Call Social Security at 800-772-1213 or download the booklets from the Social Security Web site at www.ssa.gov.

CHAPTER 31

Insurance and Estate Planning

After 50, it is important to review how your investments, insurance, and holdings will impact your estate. In this chapter, I suggest financial arrangements you might want to check, based on problems I have seen.

Wills

Many people sign their Wills without reading them thoroughly. Instead, they rely on their lawyers to tell them what is in the Will. I recommend that you dust off your Will and read it out loud to yourself. See if it clearly states what you intend. If not, you need to remedy that without delay.

Review how your holdings are titled. Is your home in your name alone? Is it in the name of your spouse and you jointly, with right of survivorship? How are your investment accounts titled? Who are the owners and beneficiaries of your life insurance policies? Who are your beneficiaries on your IRAs and what about your 401(k) plan beneficiaries? (We'll discuss some of the issues relating to these items in this chapter.) Don't rely on memory. Look at the documents and make sure they reflect your intentions.

And, if you don't have a Will, it's time to get one. Even if you think your estate is not large enough to require tax planning, you need a Will to make sure your assets pass in accordance with your wishes. To get the help you need, contact your local bar association for names of attorneys whose practices are focused on trusts and estates.

> **TIP**
>
> Dust off your Will and read it out loud to yourself!

Your Insurance

Review your life insurance coverage. Is it adequate? Or, do you need any at all? Consider the risk you are trying to cover. If you are the sole provider of a family of four and your youngest child is an infant, your risk is the loss of your income until your youngest becomes self-sufficient.

Check to see who is named as the owner of the policy. If you have insurance on your own life and you own the policy, the death benefit counts as a taxable asset of your estate. Normally, you want to avoid estate taxation of the death benefit if you can.

If you bought your life insurance policy through an insurance agent without consulting a tax- or estate-planning attorney, you may want to have your lawyer look at the ownership issue. Generally, you want the owner of the policy to be someone other than the insured. Insurance trusts are used for this purpose. But, they have to be drafted correctly and the policy has to be handled correctly. You usually want an attorney to draft the trust, even though an insurance agent or financial planner may offer to do this for you.

> **CAUTION**
>
> If you are not careful with your beneficiary designations, your estate could look a lot different than you planned.

If you do need to transfer the ownership of a policy, take time to understand how the process is to work. Read the documentation and ask questions. For example, ask how the transfer can fail and what happens if it does. What you want to avoid is an insurance trust that is ineffective.

Long-term care insurance is being aggressively marketed right now. Consider whether this type of insurance is right for you or perhaps an elder member of the family. Check your disability insurance coverage as well.

Beneficiary Designations

Check your beneficiary designations on your company savings plans and IRAs. If you are not careful with your beneficiary designations, your estate could look a lot different than you planned. When you first sign up for your company savings plan, you complete an enrollment form to indicate your contributions and investments. The enrollment form also allows you to name one or more beneficiaries.

Let's say it is a 401(k) plan. In the event of your death, the full amount of your 401(k) is included in your taxable estate and is subject to federal estate taxes and state inheritance and death taxes. Income taxes will also be due, but can be lessened through planning. But, who gets your 401(k)? Your 401(k) is distributed to the beneficiaries you name in the beneficiary designation on the enrollment form. This is so even if your Will provides otherwise.

However, there is a special rule for spouses. If you are married, your 401(k) is distributed to your surviving spouse unless he or she consents in writing to another beneficiary. Even if you name another beneficiary in your Will or in your beneficiary designation, your 401(k) will go to your surviving spouse unless he or she executes a signed waiver.

> **NOTE**
>
> If you leave your beneficiary designation blank, some plans provide that your estate will be your beneficiary if you do not provide one. This poses an income tax problem.

If you are married, you may name a beneficiary other than your spouse only with your spouse's written consent. If you leave your beneficiary designation blank, your spouse will be your beneficiary. If you are not married, you may name anyone as your beneficiary. If you leave your beneficiary designation blank, some plans provide that your estate will be your beneficiary if you do not provide one. This poses an income tax problem.

Say you named your daughter as your sole beneficiary in your Will and you left your 401(k) beneficiary designation blank. Because of a special tax rule (an estate is not a designated beneficiary under the IRC), these assets are now fully income taxable.

To preserve possible income tax deferral opportunities for your beneficiaries, you must name them in your 401(k) beneficiary designation (not in your Will). The same rule applies for Individual Retirement Accounts (IRAs).

Your 401(k) and IRA accounts are part of your estate, along with the other assets you own at death. Not all will necessarily generate an estate tax bill. A system of tax credits and deductions may lower or eliminate estate taxes depending on whom you name as your beneficiary and the size of your estate.

The best way to get an understanding of how estate taxes can affect you is to look at an example. I caution you, however, that this only illustrates the tip of the iceberg. Estate planning is a highly complex area of the law that requires the skills of a knowledgeable attorney.

Estate Taxes

To show how estate taxes might work, let's take an example that includes a 401(k) account and an insurance policy. Say you are married to a U.S. citizen and have one daughter, age 9. Your 401(k) account is worth $500,000. You own a home worth $500,000 and have life insurance for $500,000. In addition, you have an IRA of $500,000. That brings your taxable estate to $2 million. Your spouse is your beneficiary under your Will and your designated beneficiary on your 401(k) and IRA accounts.

What Happens If You Die First?

There is a special rule that applies to U.S. citizen spouses. All the assets you leave to your surviving spouse, including your 401(k) and IRA, fall under the unlimited marital deduction. The effect of the deduction is to exclude any assets you leave to your spouse from estate taxes. Special rules apply to non-U.S. citizen spouses.

Since your spouse is a U.S. citizen, everything you leave to him or her will be estate tax free. That means that your entire estate of $2 million will be free from estate taxes.

Now, say your spouse dies first and at your death, you leave all your assets to your daughter. That makes things a little more complicated. Under federal law, your $2 million estate is taxable, but not fully. $675,000 is excluded from your taxable estate for deaths occurring in 2001. The amount of the exclusion increases over time to $1 million by the year 2006. The exclusion will be available at death to the extent not used to make lifetime taxable gifts.

> **NOTE**
> Proper planning before the first spouse's death can save the family significant amounts.

Applying the exclusion and assuming no further credits, your daughter would receive about $1.5 million instead of $2 million. The difference of about $500,000 would be the approximate federal estate tax bill that would be due. In addition, state taxes would be due. However, the state taxes would offset the federal tax bill in part.

What Are the Lessons Here?

1. If you are married, your surviving spouse (U.S. citizen) will receive assets left to him or her free of estate taxes. But remember that you may have family estate-planning problems if you don't look beyond the first to die. Proper planning before the first spouse's death can save the family significant amounts. And, that may indicate a plan other than leaving everything outright to the spouse. Lifetime gifting offers additional opportunities for tax savings, as does proper use of trusts.

2. Don't assume that you are home free if your estate is less than $675,000, the federal estate tax exclusion for 2001. State taxes could be due at much lower levels.

3. Be sure to check your beneficiary designations on your IRA and 401(k) accounts. They will take precedence over your Will and can help you preserve continued income tax deferral if handled correctly.

4. There are also non-tax-planning issues to be aware of, such as trusts for children and disability planning.

5. You have a choice when it comes to estate planning. You can pay Uncle Sam or you can pay your beneficiaries. With thoughtful planning and competent legal counsel, you can protect your assets for your family.

NOTE

If you do not wish to discuss your financial matters with your children, make sure your lawyer and investment adviser, working together, help you with the organization and planning process.

Summary

While planning for subsequent generations is not a priority for many people, it is probably a worthwhile exercise to review your holdings after 50 and to organize your accounts, insurance policies, beneficiary designations, and Will. You can save your family some taxes and some headaches by doing some organizing and planning now. I have seen people go into nursing homes when they become ill unexpectedly and their children have to try to make sense of their finances. It is difficult enough for family members to deal with a loved one's illness; it is a real burden for them to try to ascertain your wishes if you have not shared them. If you do not wish to discuss your financial matters with your children, make sure your lawyer and investment adviser, working together, help you with the organization and planning process.

CHAPTER 32

Where to Go from Here

In writing this book, my goals have been to give you special issues to think about, familiarize you with resources that are both sound and easy to use, and perhaps save you from making mistakes. At this point, you probably want to take the next step. Here are my recommendations.

If you are saving from earnings and have been investing successfully for a long time, you will likely continue on course while making a few adjustments. Watch your investments regularly and weed out those that do not further your investment objectives or that are not performing as you would like. As you approach retirement, you may wish to begin carefully restructuring a part of your portfolio for income production.

If you are still working and are behind in building capital for your retirement, consider this a wake-up call. What are you waiting for? Start a regular program of investing. Take full advantage of employer-sponsored savings plans, especially if your plan has a match or profit-sharing contribution. Since compounding needs time to develop, the sooner you begin, the better off you will be. Just like starting a diet, you don't want to wait until tomorrow. You want to start now.

If you have just received a large sum of money from an inheritance, divorce settlement, pension distribution, buyout, or other source, you are particularly vulnerable to making a serious mistake. You need to take special care before doing anything with your money that can tie it up or expose it to undue risk. This is not a time to let your ego get in the way of the facts. Remember my story about the economist in Chapter 10. Finding himself in this position, he put a very large sum of money into an investment he did not understand, based on an oral promise that the investment was guaranteed not to lose money. No matter what kind of opportunity is presented to you, if it is worthwhile, it will be available a few days later—after you have read that prospectus and asked those tough questions discussed at the end of Chapter 19. Do not let anyone rush you into making a decision until you are ready. Do not buy anything that you cannot explain to a friend. Do not buy anything that sounds too good to be true. Do not buy anything from a fast-talking solicitor who calls you at home at dinnertime.

Due in part to inheritances and the 401(k) plan, many people who don't think of themselves as wealthy may find themselves with tens of thousands or hundreds of thousands of dollars—even millions of dollars—to invest, some for the first time in their lives. Irrespective of the dollar amount, if the sum is important to you, it deserves care and attention. Risky investing or lack of care can jeopardize assets you will not be able to replace in the same way you acquired them. This is a time for extra thought and caution. Reading books such as this one and those mentioned in Appendix A is a good start. Becoming more skeptical also helps. Not being afraid to ask embarrassing questions also works to your advantage. Asking for promises to be put in writing won't make you popular, but it will deter those who can't keep those promises.

As you move forward, you will discover that structuring a portfolio is a very personal exercise, as it should be. Your circumstances will differ from those of other people. Your current holdings, income, pension benefits, and expenses—and your needs, experience, knowledge, skill, time horizon, whom you choose to work with, and even your personality to a degree—will dictate how you approach investing and to some extent, your success at achieving the results you desire. What you seek to achieve and how you go about that process will shape your experience. If you seek overly optimistic results for your circumstances, you may find yourself taking on too much risk. If you are too cautious, you may find that your returns don't keep you ahead of inflation and taxes.

Commit to taking your time and using your better judgment. It's your money. It's your future. It's your job to take an interest and to guide your portfolio to where it needs to go. Remember that you are not trying to outperform anyone. You are trying to do your best considering your circumstances. If you just believe in your own good judgment, you can do what it takes to succeed.

NEXT STEPS

If you do not have a set of investment objectives, now is a good time to write them down. Just in case you're thinking of skipping this step, let me remind you that investment objectives are covered in no fewer than seven chapters (Chapters 5, 7, 8, 15, 20, 21, and 25). Yes, I do think this is important. And, no, it will not take long. At a minimum, you need to understand the demands you will be placing on your portfolio.

Since most people will need to produce income from their portfolios at some time in their lives, the investment objective I want to explore with you here is income production.

QUESTIONS TO ASK YOURSELF

Do you need money for living expenses right now? If the answer is yes, one of your investment objectives is to produce "current income."

How much cash flow do you need per year? For illustration purposes, say that's $24,000 a year.

How much of your portfolio do you want to commit to this purpose? Using the Demands-Based Formula at the end of Chapter 6, figure out the capital you would need to commit to income production at low-risk levels and at high-risk levels. For illustration purposes, I am using 5 percent for low risk: $24,000 of income needed, divided by .05 (which is the yield I am assuming for low-risk Treasury bills) = $480,000 of capital I would need to commit. For high risk, I am using 10 percent: $24,000 of income needed, divided by .10, which is the yield I am assuming for high-risk, high-yield bonds = $240,000 of capital.

That gives me a range of $240,000 to $480,000. If you calculate the Demands-Based Formula for yourself and find that you do not have enough capital to produce the income you need, even at the highest level of risk, you will not be able to use income-producing investments to meet your needs; instead, you will need to sell off capital as you need it.

(continued)

How long will you need this cash flow? Let's say this is retirement income, and you will need it for the rest of your life.

At this point, write down: *"As to between $240,000 and $480,000 of my capital, my investment objective is to produce current income of $24,000 a year for the rest of my life, increasing over time to offset loss of purchasing power due to inflation."* If you are not ready to do a Demands-Based Asset calculation, write this down: *"For a yet to be determined part of my capital, my investment objective is to produce current income of $24,000 a year for the rest of my life, increasing over time to offset loss of purchasing power due to inflation."*

Next, narrow the asset range ($240,000–$480,000) you need to commit, leaving the inflation issue for later. In this illustration, $240,000 assumes a very high level of risk, which I would not recommend, and $480,000 assumes a very low level of risk. How do you know which way to go? More importantly, *what if you have insufficient assets for one or the other or both?*

If you feel you are too new to investing to make a good judgment on this issue, it's always best to assume less risk, which would mean committing more assets. This is also true if you are more experienced, but are in a painful transition in life. Perhaps you were recently widowed or divorced, or terminated from your job. Under those circumstances, protect your principal by taking less risk. Later, when the crisis passes, things will look different and you don't want to have losses to worry about.

If you are working with an adviser, have him or her make a recommendation, but be sure that you fully understand the risk level recommended and the long-term plan. If I were advising you, I would want to know the rest of your story before making any recommendations: your financial circumstances and your experience, including how you dealt with credit, market, and other risks in the past; whether you have invested in fixed income instruments or stocks, and under what circumstances; how you deal with paper losses; and so on. Then, based on your answers, your circumstances, and the current state of the markets, I would recommend how to produce this income for you. Together, we would then review what we could expect from that portfolio and decide on a course of action. At this time, we would also assess whether your assets were sufficient to create the needed cash flow using income-producing instruments, and what other alternatives presented themselves.

What if you wanted to raise the $24,000 by selling off capital instead of investing for income? Then your investment objective would read something like this: *"For a yet to be determined part of my capital, my investment objective is to produce cash flow from selling $24,000 of my holdings* *each year for the rest of my life, increasing this amount over time to offset loss of purchasing power due to inflation."*

Next, commit to an approach. Let's say you arrive at $360,000 for a mid-risk bond portfolio that yields 7.5 percent to achieve your $24,000 of desired current income. Refine your objectives as follows: *"As to $360,000 of my capital, my investment objective is to produce current income of $24,000 a year for the rest of my life, increasing over time to offset loss of purchasing power due to inflation."*

After making this commitment, you can then deal with the rest of your asset picture. You will need an element of growth in your portfolio to offset inflation and you should also have a portion committed to preservation of capital for safety and for emergencies. The allocation between the two will be subjective. Here is an example: "I will split the remainder of my assets into two portions, one for growth and one for preservation of capital. I will commit 75 percent for capital appreciation in equity investments and 25 percent for preservation of capital in money market investments."

This first step will get you focused on a possible course of action, or will tell you that you cannot go in a certain direction. It may tell you that you have insufficient assets to retire on and need to work longer, spend less, or sell off your capital over time. After having a sense of direction, then you can select appropriate investments to meet those objectives. You may find it helpful to revisit the chapters on risk and the markets first (Chapters 2 and 3), and the chapters on selecting investments for capital appreciation (Chapters 12, 13, 14, and 15), income (Chapter 16), and preservation of capital (Chapter 17). Also be sure to factor in taxes as discussed at the end of Chapter 6 (page 32).

Recommended Resources

If you have significant assets that need managing, I recommend you avoid the fluff and concentrate on the following starred classics. They are excellent references for general background. The books that are not starred are textbooks that cover specific issues.

Cottle, Sidney, Roger F. Murray, and Frank E. Block. *Graham and Dodd's Security Analysis, Fifth Edition.* New York: McGraw-Hill, 1988.

Darst, David M. *The Complete Bond Book.* New York: McGraw-Hill, 1975.

de La Grandville, Olivier. *Bond Pricing and Portfolio Analysis.* Cambridge, MA: MIT Press, 2001.

*Engel, Louis, and Henry R. Hecht. *How to Buy Stocks, Eighth Edition.* New York: Little, Brown, 1994.

Fabozzi, Frank J. *The Handbook of Fixed Income Securities, Third Edition.* Homewood, IL: Business One Irwin, 1983.

*Fabozzi, Frank J. *Investment Management.* Englewood Cliffs, NJ: Prentice Hall, 1995.

Francis, Jack Clark, and Avner Wolf. *The Handbook of Interest Rate Risk Management.* Burr Ridge, IL: Irwin, 1994.

Fredman, Albert J., and Russ Wiles. *How Mutual Funds Work.* New York: New York Institute of Finance, 1993.

*Graham, Benjamin. *The Intelligent Investor, Fourth Revised Edition.* New York: Harper & Row, 1973.

*Graham, Benjamin, David L. Dodd, and Sidney Cottle. *Security Analysis, Fourth Edition.* New York: McGraw-Hill, 1962.

Lamb, Robert, and Stephen P. Rappaport. *The Comprehensive Review of Tax-Exempt Securities and Public Finance.* New York: McGraw-Hill, 1980.

*Leffler, George L., and Loring C. Farwell. *The Stock Market, Third Edition.* New York: Ronald Press, 1963.

*Loeb, G.M. *The Battle for Investment Survival.* New York: Simon and Schuster, 1957.

Maginn, John L., and Donald L. Tuttle. *Managing Investment Portfolios, A Dynamic Process, Second Edition.* Boston, MA: Warren, Gorham & Lamont, 1990.

*Markowitz, Harry M. *Portfolio Selection.* Cambridge, MA: Blackwell, 1996.

New York Institute of Finance. *How the Bond Market Works.* New York: New York Institute of Finance, 1988.

*O'Neil, William J. *24 Essential Lessons for Investment Success.* New York: McGraw-Hill, 2000.

Pistolese, Clifford. *The Investor's Self-Teaching Seminars: Using Technical Analysis.* Chicago, IL: Probus, 1989.

*Sharpe, William F., Gordon J. Alexander, and Jeffery V. Bailey. *Investments, Sixth Edition.* Upper Saddle River, NJ: Prentice Hall, 1999.

Stephens, Jack. *Avoiding the Tax Traps in Your IRA.* Fulton, TX: Legalaction Publications, 1999.

Thomsett, Michael C. *The Mathematics of Investing.* New York: John Wiley & Sons, 1989.

Trone, Donald B., William R. Albright, and Philip R. Taylor. *The Management of Investment Decisions.* Chicago, IL: Irwin, 1996.

The following organizations also provide information on investing.

American Association of Individual Investors (AAII) specializes in providing education in the area of stock investing, mutual funds, portfolio management, and retirement planning. For more information, visit their Web site at www.aaii.com or call 800-428-2244.

Brentmark of Orlando provides software IRA distribution software using the new tax rules discussed in Chapters 28 and 29. This software is useful to tax and finance professionals in planning distributions from their IRAs and other tax deferred accounts. For more information, call 800-879-6665 or visit their Web site at www.brentmark.com.

Ibbotson Associates, established by Professor Roger Ibbotson in 1977, offers consulting and training services as well as software, data, and presentation products. For more information, visit their Web site at www.ibbotson.com.

Morningstar, based in Chicago, is the leading provider of mutual fund, stock, and variable-insurance investment information, including data, analysis, and editorial commentary. For more information, visit their Web site at www.morningstar.com or call 800-735-0700.

National Association of Investors Corporation (NAIC) is a nonprofit association dedicated to investment education. It is the leading association for the investment club movement in the United States. Since 1951, NAIC's mission has been to provide a program of sound investment information, education, and support that helps create successful, lifetime investors. For more information, visit their Web site at www.naic.com or call 877-275-6242.

Standard & Poor's Select Funds research is a unique way to identify the top mutual funds in each investment style category. Applying the resources of one of the world's premier financial research organizations, Standard & Poor's identifies funds that have generated a consistently strong track record and are well managed. No other mutual fund research incorporates such a comprehensive review of management or focuses on consistency of performance in its evaluations. For further information about Standard & Poor's Select Funds, go to www.standardandpoors.com/onfunds.

Steele Systems offers *The Steele Mutual Fund Expert*, an intuitive, easy-to-use software for mutual fund selection, tracking, analysis, and presentation. Data is supplied by *Standard & Poor's Micropal*. For more information, visit their Web site at www.steelesystems .com or call 800-678-3863.

Value Line (started in 1931) is best known for *The Value Line Investment Survey*, a comprehensive source of information and advice on approximately 1,700 stocks. For more information, visit their Web site at www.valueline.com or call 800-634-3583.

About the Author

JULIE JASON is a personal money manager with 25 years of experience in the investment industry, starting her career on Wall Street as a securities attorney. Ms. Jason manages "irreplaceable assets" for clients of Jackson, Grant, an investment firm she cofounded 10 years ago. Ms. Jason serves as an arbitrator for the New York Stock Exchange and the National Association of Securities Dealers.

A proponent of reasoned investment policy, Ms. Jason has appeared on national and local radio and television programs such as NBC Nightly News, CNNfn, CNBC, and National Public Radio and has been quoted in such publications as *Business Week*, *Money Magazine*, the *New York Times*, and *The Boston Globe*. Ms. Jason writes and speaks on investment topics and teaches investment principles in continuing education programs for attorneys and accountants as well as programs for the general public. Her weekly investment column, which originated in the *Stamford Advocate* and *Greenwich Time*, is distributed worldwide by United Media, headquartered in New York. Ms. Jason is the author of *You and Your 401(k): How to Maximize Your Returns*, a guide for 401(k) participants, and *The 401(k) Plan Handbook*, a guide for corporate officers who are responsible for their company 401(k) plans.

Ms. Jason welcomes reader questions addressed to her c/o Jackson, Grant, 1177 High Ridge Road, Stamford, CT 06905 or e-mailed to jj@JulieJason.com.

Index